THE LEBANESE KITCHEN

THE
LEBANESE KITCHEN
QUICK & HEALTHY RECIPES

Monique Bassila Zaarour

Interlink Books

An imprint of Interlink Publishing Group, Inc.
Northampton, Massachusetts

I dedicate this book to all the women in my family starting with my dear mother Antoinette and to all my sisters: Denise, Hilda, Claude, Nathalie, and especially Nadine; ending with my adorable daughter Maria who completed the joy of my existence. Thank you all for being such an important part of my life. Many thanks to: Christine Aoun, Habib Malek, Ghaleb Solh and Sabine Taoukjian.

First published in 2007 by

INTERLINK BOOKS
An imprint of Interlink Publishing Group, Inc.
46 Crosby Street, Northampton, MA 01060
www.interlinkbooks.com

ISBN: 1-56656-642-8 (hardback)
ISBN 13: 978-1-56656-642-1

Printed and bound in China

To request our complete 40-page full-color catalog, please call us toll free at **1-800-238-LINK**, visit our website at **www.interlinkbooks.com** or write to
Interlink Publishing
46 Crosby Street, Northampton, MA 01060
e-mail: info@interlinkbooks.com

Introduction

I am a Canadian registered dietitian with Lebanese roots. I used my knowledge of nutrition and my cultural background to uncover the nutritional value of Lebanese cuisine and appreciate its adequacy. Lebanese dishes, if cooked in a healthy way, comply with the requirements and guidelines of healthy eating. They are rich in vegetables, legumes, and fibers, moderate in meat and chicken.

Being a working mother myself, I am often asked how I find the time to prepare the food without resorting to commercial fast-food solutions. The secret is very simple: it starts with believing in the importance of healthy cooking, and refusing, as a mother, to fall prey to the fast-food industry. I am very well aware of the importance of healthy food and the fact that people, especially children, are not just getting heavier, they are getting heavier fast. In the United States, for instance, where child obesity is emerging as a major problem, the percentage of children who are overweight has doubled in the last 20 years.

The Lebanese Kitchen contains 65 quick recipes with comprehensive indications of every recipe's nutritional information: calories, cholesterol, fat, carbohydrates, proteins, fibers, vitamins, minerals, and phytochemicals. This book is intended for the entire family. It is also suitable for people who suffer from high cholesterol or other health problems such as heart disease, blood pressure and diabetes.

The book begins in a user-friendly way with a section on the prior preparation of necessary ingredients in order to ease the daily task of cooking. It is then divided into four chapters: Soups & Salads, Vegetarian, Beef Platters, and Chicken & Fish. Read the recipe notes and tips, which will make cooking the highlight of the day.

What I am hoping to provide in this book is a much-needed guide to organize your kitchen, as well as an approach to sensible, enjoyable, and healthy Lebanese cooking at home that will not take more than half an hour to prepare.

Efficient, nutritious, healthy and delicious meals are the goal of this book. Isn't this every cook's dream?

Measurements

1 quart = 4 cups
1 cup = 8 ounces
1 tablespoon = 1/2 fluid ounce

Note: The quantities of salt in the recipes are
moderate and can be modified according to taste.

Preparation Time
Is the time required to prepare the ingredients.
It does not include prior preparation or cooking time.

Cooking Time
Is the time required for the dish to be cooked.

Soaking Time
Is the time needed to soak a specific ingredient in
water or to marinate it in a certain sauce.

Contents

Prior Preparation

In this chapter there are 7 basic recipes, which I advise you to prepare and freeze once every month or as needed. The whole idea of this cookbook is based on this chapter because having these ingredients on hand will speed up and ease the process of daily cooking. After completion of each recipe, you should:

• Divide the food and place it in special bags or containers for the freezer.
• Press the containers or bags well to get rid of all air inside.
• Tag the containers or bags with their contents and the date when placed in the freezer.
• Place the new foods at the back and the previously prepared ones at the front of the freezer.
• Defrost the food in the fridge 24 hours before cooking, or immediately in the microwave, or under cold running water.
• Avoid defrosting in hot water or outside the fridge, which could cause the growth of bacteria and might, in some cases, result in food poisoning.

COOKED CUBED BEEF

INGREDIENTS

1 serving

1/2 pound lean beef, cut into 3/4-inch cubes
1 cup water
1 pinch salt
1 pinch allspice
1 pinch cinnamon
1/2 Bouquet (see below)

8 servings

4 pounds lean beef, cut into 3/4-inch cubes
5 cups water
1 teaspoon salt
1 teaspoon allspice
1 teaspoon cinnamon
1 Bouquet:
  2 cinnamon sticks
  4 cardamom seeds
  2 bay leaves
  1 medium onion, quartered
  1/2 small lemon

PREPARATION

In a nonstick pan, cook cubed beef over medium heat. Stir constantly for 10 minutes or until lightly browned.
Add water and bring to a boil; skim surface of water with slotted spoon.
Add seasonings.
Wrap contents of Bouquet in cheesecloth and tie closed, then add to meat. Cover pan and cook over low heat for 20 minutes.
Remove Bouquet and keep the cubed beef and its broth for later use.

Tip: Prepare 8 servings and divide them into equal parts of 1/2 pound (and 1/2 cup of broth), for later use in several recipes. They can be kept in the freezer for 2 months. Defrost the beef in the fridge 24 hours before use, or immediately in the microwave, or under cold running water.

COOKED GROUND BEEF

INGREDIENTS

1 serving

5 1/4 ounces lean ground beef
1/2 onion, finely chopped
1 pinch allspice
1 pinch cinnamon
1 pinch salt

14 servings

4 pounds lean ground beef
6 onions, finely chopped
1 teaspoon allspice
1 teaspoon cinnamon
2 teaspoons salt

PREPARATION

In a nonstick pan, cook ground beef over medium heat, stirring constantly using a flat wooden spoon until lightly browned. Make sure the beef doesn't stick together.
Add onions and seasonings. Stir for 15 more minutes or until all water evaporates.

Tip: Prepare 14 servings and divide them into equal parts. Put them in aluminum foil, bags, or containers in the freezer for later use in several recipes. They can be kept in the freezer for 2 months. Defrost the ground beef in the fridge 24 hours before use, or immediately in the microwave,or under cold running water.
You can use 2 servings instead of kafta meat in several recipes.

CILANTRO AND GARLIC

INGREDIENTS

1 serving

1/2 bunch cilantro
5 garlic cloves
1 pinch salt

20 servings

10 bunches cilantro
10 garlic bulbs
1 tablespoon salt

PREPARATION

Chop cilantro using a food processor or
by hand.
Crush garlic with salt using a food processor
or by hand.
In a nonstick pan, stir garlic and cilantro
continuously over low heat for 15 minutes or
until tender.

Tip: Prepare 20 servings and divide them into equal
parts for later use in several recipes.
The servings can be kept in the freezer for 3 months.

CRUSHED GARLIC

INGREDIENTS

10 garlic bulbs or as needed

PREPARATION

Peel garlic and crush into a paste using a food processor or by hand.

Tip: Crush 10 garlic bulbs and divide them equally for later use in several recipes. Place immediately in the freezer. If garlic turns greenish in color, it does not lose any of its nutritional value.
Every 2 crushed cloves = 1/2 teaspoon.
They can be kept in the freezer for 3 months.

BOILED LEGUMES

INGREDIENTS

1 serving

1 cup dried legumes of your choice
Water as needed

5 servings

5 cups dried legumes of your choice
Water as needed

PREPARATION

Soak legumes in water for 12 hours (skip this step if using lentils).
Drain well and put in a stockpot.
Cover with water. Bring to a boil.
Cook over low heat for 1 hour (or 30 minutes in a pressure cooker). Allow to cool.

Tip: Prepare 5 servings and divide them into equal parts (2 or more cups of drained cooked legumes with 1/2 cup of the cooking liquid). Put them in special containers or bags in the freezer for later use in several recipes. They can be kept in the freezer for 2 months. Defrost cooked legumes 24 hours in the fridge before use.
1 cup dried legumes = 2 1/2 cups drained cooked legumes.

TOASTED PINE NUTS

INGREDIENTS

Pine nuts, 1 to 8 cups (as needed)

PREPARATION

Put pine nuts on a nonstick baking sheet in a preheated oven (475°) for 20 minutes.
Shake every 5 minutes for even toasting.

Tip: Prepare 8 cups pine nuts and put in the freezer for later use in several recipes.
The pine nuts can be kept in the freezer for 5 months.

BOILED CHICKEN AND BROTH

INGREDIENTS

1 serving

1 pound chicken breast
1 quart water or as needed
1/2 Bouquet (p.8)
1 pinch salt
1 pinch allspice
1 pinch cinnamon
1 pinch white pepper

4 servings

4 pounds chicken breast
4 quarts water or as needed
1 Bouquet (p.8)
1 teaspoon salt
1 teaspoon allspice
1 teaspoon cinnamon
1 teaspoon white pepper

PREPARATION

Put chicken and water in a stockpot.
Bring to a boil.
Skim surface of water with a slotted spoon.
Wrap and tie contents of Bouquet in cheesecloth, then add to chicken with seasonings.
Cook for 1 hour over low heat.
Remove Bouquet and keep the chicken and its broth for later use.

Tip: Prepare 4 servings and divide chicken and broth separately into equal parts for later use in several recipes. They can be kept in the freezer for 1 month. Defrost in the fridge 24 hours before use, or immediately in the microwave, or under cold running water.

Soups & Salads

Lebanese soups and salads are considered highly nutritious, simple to prepare and easy to digest. They are rich in vegetables and legumes.

Vegetables, especially the darker ones, are considered a very important source of vitamins, minerals, and phytochemicals. They are low in calories, fat free, cholesterol free, and rich in fiber. Vegetables, in general, lower the risk of obesity, heart disease, and cancer.

The nutritional content of vegetables decreases gradually with time after harvest. Therefore, it is best to consume the freshest possible vegetables. Frozen or canned vegetables are preserved fresh within 24 hours of harvest, while they are still at their peak of nutritional content. However, canned vegetables, as a result of preservation in water, lose some of their nutritional elements, especially water-soluble vitamins. Frozen vegetables, on the other hand, keep most of their nutrients and they regain their original texture, flavor, and color after cooking.

Vegetables, regardless of their source, are best cooked in a small amount of water and over high heat in a covered container. For quick and easy cooking, use canned tomatoes with their liquid and frozen vegetables.

For more information on the nutritional value of legumes, see page 39.

TABBOULEH

serves 5 | preparation time 30 min

INGREDIENTS

1 small onion, finely chopped
1 teaspoon salt
1/2 teaspoon allspice
1/2 teaspoon sumac

3 bunches parsley leaves, finely chopped
5 small tomatoes, finely diced
2 ribs mint leaves, finely chopped
2 tablespoons fine bulgur, rinsed and
    drained

5 tablespoons lemon juice
5 tablespoons olive oil

Tip: The parsley should not be wet while chopping.
You can chop the parsley using a knife or on high speed in a food processor.

PREPARATION

Mix salt, allspice, and sumac, then rub onions in the mixture, coating them thoroughly.

Add remaining vegetables and mix. Add bulgur; mix again.

Add lemon juice and olive oil. Mix gently until evenly distributed.

Serve cold.

NUTRITIONAL VALUE PER SERVING

Energy (Cal)	200
Cholesterol (mg)	0
Fat (g)	13
Carbohydrate (g)	18
Protein (g)	4
Fiber (g)	6

Rich in fiber and vitamin C.
Contains carotenoids (pp.126–133).

FATTOUSH

serves 5 | preparation time 25 min

INGREDIENTS

1 large onion, thinly sliced
1 tablespoon sumac
2 large tomatoes, diced
4 cucumbers, diced
1/4 bunch mint leaves, chopped
1/2 bunch parsley leaves
1 bunch watercress leaves
10 lettuce leaves, shredded
5 radishes, sliced in rounds
1 medium loaf pita bread, toasted

Dressing
2 garlic cloves, crushed
1 teaspoon salt
3 tablespoons red-wine or grape vinegar
5 tablespoons olive oil

PREPARATION

Rub onions in sumac, coating them
thoroughly.
Add vegetables gradually and mix well.
Cut bread into small squares.
Mix half of the bread with vegetables.

In a separate bowl, mix dressing ingredients.
Add to vegetables and mix gently until
evenly distributed.

Serve cold.
Garnish with remaining bread.

NUTRITIONAL VALUE PER SERVING

Energy (Cal)	225
Cholesterol (mg)	0
Fat (g)	14
Carbohydrate (g)	21
Protein (g)	4
Fiber (g)	3

Rich in folate, unsaturated fat, and vitamin C (pp.126–133).

NUTRITIONAL VALUE PER SERVING

Rich in fiber and vitamin C (pp.126–133).

Energy (Cal)	190
Cholesterol (mg)	0
Fat (g)	14
Carbohydrate (g)	14
Protein (g)	2
Fiber (g)	2

EGGPLANT SALAD

serves **4** | preparation time **15 min** | cooking time **6 min**

INGREDIENTS

1 large eggplant
1 small onion, finely chopped
2 medium tomatoes, finely diced

Dressing
1 garlic clove, crushed
1 teaspoon yellow mustard
1/2 teaspoon salt
1 pinch white pepper
1 teaspoon dried mint
2 tablespoons red-wine or grape vinegar
2 tablespoons lemon juice
4 tablespoons olive oil

PREPARATION

Peel eggplant; wrap it with plastic wrap.
Cook in microwave for 6 minutes.
Unwrap eggplant and cut into small cubes.
Mix with onions and tomatoes.

In a separate bowl, mix garlic with mustard.
Add remaining ingredients and mix again.
Add to vegetables and mix gently until
evenly distributed.

Serve cold.

GREEN BEAN SALAD

serves 5 | preparation time 5 min | cooking time 15 min

INGREDIENTS

2 pounds frozen green beans
2 cups water

Dressing
2 garlic cloves, crushed
1 teaspoon salt
4 tablespoons lemon juice
5 tablespoons olive oil

PREPARATION

In a large saucepan, cook green beans in water over medium heat until tender. Drain and put in serving bowl.

Mix dressing ingredients in a small bowl. Pour over green beans and mix until evenly distributed.

Serve hot or cold.

Tip: Vegetables should be cooked for a short time in a small amount of water to preserve their nutrients. You can use 3 pounds fresh green beans, cut into 2-inch pieces.

NUTRITIONAL VALUE PER SERVING

Energy (Cal)	210
Cholesterol (mg)	0
Fat (g)	14
Carbohydrate (g)	17
Protein (g)	4
Fiber (g)	7

Rich in fiber and vitamin C.
Contains carotenoids and isoflavone (pp.126–133).

NUTRITIONAL VALUE PER SERVING

Rich in fiber, folate, potassium, and vitamin B6.
Contains isoflavone (pp.126–133).

Energy (Cal)	360
Cholesterol (mg)	0
Fat (g)	15
Carbohydrate (g)	42
Protein (g)	15
Fiber (g)	14

KIDNEY BEAN SALAD

serves **4** | preparation time **5 min** | cooking time **15 min**

INGREDIENTS

2 cups water
4 cups cooked kidney beans (p.12)

Dressing
2 garlic cloves, crushed
1/2 teaspoon salt
1 pinch red pepper
1 pinch dried mint
5 tablespoons lemon juice
4 tablespoons olive oil

PREPARATION

In a large saucepan, bring water to a boil. Add kidney beans over medium heat until tender. Put in a large bowl with some of their cooking liquid.

In a small bowl, mix all dressing ingredients. Add to kidney beans and mix gently until evenly distributed.
Add more olive oil if desired.

Serve hot with fresh tomatoes and onions.

Tip: If kidney beans were uncooked, start by boiling 1 1/2 cups dried kidney beans (p.12), or use canned kidney beans.
You can use any kind of kidney beans.

Ful Mudammas fava bean salad

NUTRITIONAL VALUE PER SERVING

Energy (Cal)	460
Cholesterol (mg)	0
Fat (g)	19
Carbohydrate (g)	53
Protein (g)	19
Fiber (g)	11

Rich in fiber, folate, magnesium, and vitamin C.
Contains tannins (pp.126–133).

Balila chickpea salad

NUTRITIONAL VALUE PER SERVING

Energy (Cal)	415
Cholesterol (mg)	0
Fat (g)	17
Carbohydrate (g)	50
Protein (g)	16
Fiber (g)	6

Rich in fiber, folate, and magnesium.
Contains tannins (pp.126–133).

FUL MUDAMMAS fava bean salad

serves 3 | preparation time 5 min | cooking time 15 min

INGREDIENTS

2 cups water
4 cups cooked black fava beans (p.12)

4 garlic cloves, crushed (p.11)
1 teaspoon salt
1/2 cup lemon juice

1/4 bunch parsley, finely chopped
4 tablespoons olive oil

Tip: If fava beans were uncooked, start by boiling
1 1/2 cups dried fava beans (p.12) or use canned fava
beans.

PREPARATION

In a large saucepan, bring water to a boil.
Add fava beans and cook over medium heat
until tender. Put in a large bowl with some of
their cooking liquid.

In a small bowl, mix garlic, salt, and lemon
juice.
Add to beans and mix well.

Garnish with chopped parsley and olive oil.

Serve hot with fresh onions and tomatoes.

BALILA chickpea salad

serves 4 | preparation time 5 min | cooking time 15 min

INGREDIENTS

2 cups water
4 cups cooked chickpeas (p.12)

4 garlic cloves, crushed (p.11)
1 teaspoon salt
1/2 cup lemon juice
4 tablespoons olive oil

1 pinch ground cumin

Tip: If chickpeas were uncooked, start by boiling
1 1/2 cups dried chickpeas (p.12) or use canned
chickpeas.

PREPARATION

In a large saucepan, bring water to a boil.
Add chickpeas and cook over medium heat
until tender. Put in a large bowl with some
of their cooking liquid.

In a small bowl, mix garlic, salt, lemon
juice, and olive oil.
Add to chickpeas and mix well.

Sprinkle cumin over chickpeas and serve
hot.

POTATO
AND EGG SALAD

serves **4** | preparation time **10 min** | soaking time **30 min** | cooking time **30 min**

INGREDIENTS

Dressing
1 teaspoon yellow mustard
1 teaspoon salt
1/4 teaspoon black pepper
2 tablespoons red-wine or grape vinegar
4 tablespoons lemon juice
2 tablespoons olive oil

4 medium potatoes, boiled and diced

1 medium onion, thinly sliced
3 eggs, hard-boiled and sliced in rounds
1 tablespoon parsley leaves, finely chopped

PREPARATION

In a large bowl, mix all dressing ingredients.

Add potatoes, mix slowly and marinate for 30 minutes.

Add onions and mix again.
Garnish with eggs and parsley.

Serve cold.

Tip: Potatoes are more nutritious if kept unpeeled because their skin is very rich in fiber, vitamins, and minerals.

NUTRITIONAL VALUE PER SERVING

Energy (Cal)	290
Cholesterol (mg)	185
Fat (g)	12
Carbohydrate (g)	36
Protein (g)	9
Fiber (g)	3

Rich in folate, unsaturated fat, and vitamins B6 and C.
Contains lutein (pp.126–133).

NUTRITIONAL VALUE PER SERVING

Energy (Cal)	215
Cholesterol (mg)	0
Fat (g)	3
Carbohydrate (g)	37
Protein (g)	10
Fiber (g)	7

Rich in fiber, folate, magnesium, potassium
and vitamins B6 and C.
Contains tannins (pp.126–133).

ADAS BE HAMOD
sour vegetable and lentil soup

serves 6 | preparation time 25 min | cooking time 40 min

INGREDIENTS

1 tablespoon vegetable oil
1 medium onion, finely chopped
1 serving Cilantro and Garlic (p.10)

2 cups cooked lentils (p.12)
8 cups water
1 pound chard, shredded
2 medium zucchinis, diced
2 medium potatoes, diced

1/2 cup lemon juice
1 pinch allspice
1 teaspoon salt
2 teaspoons dried cilantro

PREPARATION

In a large stockpot, heat oil. Add onions and
stir-fry until lightly browned.
Add Cilantro and Garlic and stir well.

Add lentils, water, and vegetables.
Bring to a boil. Cook over low heat until
vegetables are tender.

Add lemon juice and seasonings.
Cook for 10 more minutes over low heat
or until mixture thickens.

Serve hot.

Tip: If lentils were uncooked, start by boiling 3/4 cup dried lentils (p.12).

NUTRITIONAL VALUE PER SERVING

Energy (Cal)	325
Cholesterol (mg)	0
Fat (g)	4
Carbohydrate (g)	55
Protein (g)	17
Fiber (g)	18

Rich in complete proteins, folate, fiber, and vitamin K.
Contains isoflavone (pp.126–133).

MAKHLUTA mixed bean soup

serves **6** | preparation time **10 min** | cooking time **60 min**

INGREDIENTS

1/2 cup dried white kidney beans
1/2 cup dried red beans
1/4 cup dried black fava beans
1/2 cup dried chickpeas
1/4 cup dried big black lentils
2 quarts water

1 tablespoon vegetable oil
2 medium onions, finely chopped
1/4 cup coarse bulgur
1/4 cup short-grain rice
1/2 teaspoon cumin
1 teaspoon salt

4 tablespoons lemon juice

Tip: Cook large quantities of mixed beans and freeze them for later use.
This dish is served as a soup.

PREPARATION

Soak all beans (except lentils) in water for 12 hours, then drain.
Put lentils and beans (except fava beans) in a pressure cooker.
Cover with water, and cook over high heat. Bring to a boil.
Lower heat and cook for 30 more minutes.
Cook fava beans separately using the same method; drain and add to the other beans (do not add cooking liquid).

In a large stockpot, heat oil, add onions and stir-fry until browned.
Add to beans with bulgur, rice, and seasonings.
Cook over low heat, stirring occasionally for 30 minutes or until rice is tender.

Add lemon juice; cook over low heat for 5 more minutes.

Serve hot.

RISHTA lentil soup with pasta

serves **4** | preparation time **10 min** | cooking time **30 min**

INGREDIENTS

1 tablespoon vegetable oil
1 large onion, finely chopped
2 garlic cloves, crushed (p.11)

2 cups cooked lentils (p.12)
6 cups water
3 1/2 ounces tagliatelle
1 serving Cilantro and Garlic (p.10)
4 tablespoons lemon juice
1 teaspoon salt

PREPARATION

In a large stockpot, heat oil, add onions and stir-fry until lightly browned.
Add garlic and stir-fry for 2 more minutes.

Add lentils and water. Bring to a boil.
Add remaining ingredients and mix well.
Cook over low heat for 30 minutes or until mixture thickens.

Serve hot.

Tip: If lentils were uncooked, start by boiling 3/4 cup dried lentils (p.12).

NUTRITIONAL VALUE PER SERVING

Energy (Cal)	275
Cholesterol (mg)	0
Fat (g)	4
Carbohydrate (g)	46
Protein (g)	14
Fiber (g)	6

Rich in folate, fiber, and vitamin C.
Contains tannins (pp.126–133).

NUTRITIONAL VALUE PER SERVING

Rich in calcium, fiber, and vitamins B6 and B12 (pp.126–133).

Energy (Cal)	375
Cholesterol (mg)	45
Fat (g)	11
Carbohydrate (g)	50
Protein (g)	19
Fiber (g)	10

KESHEK traditional lebanese soup

serves **4** | preparation time **5 min** | cooking time **10 min**

INGREDIENTS

1 teaspoon vegetable oil
1 small onion, finely chopped
5 garlic cloves, crushed (p.11)
1 serving Cooked Ground Beef (p.9)
1 cup keshek powder
4 cups water
1 pinch dried mint

PREPARATION

In a large stockpot, heat oil, add onions and stir-fry until lightly browned.
Add garlic and stir-fry for 2 more minutes.
Add Cooked Ground Beef (p.9) and keshek powder.
Stir for 1 minute until keshek becomes lightly brown.
Add water gradually, stirring quickly to dissolve all keshek powder. Bring to a boil.
Cook over low heat, stirring constantly, for 5 minutes or until mixture thickens.
Sprinkle mint over soup.

Salt to taste and serve hot.

Tip: If the meat was not previously prepared, start by cooking 5 1/2 ounces uncooked ground beef (p.9). Keshek powder is found at Middle Eastern food stores.

CHICKEN SOUP

serves 5 | preparation time 5 min | cooking time 35 min

INGREDIENTS

1 pound boiled chicken, cut in strips (p.13)
6 cups chicken broth (p.13)
1 teaspoon salt
1/2 teaspoon white pepper
1 pound mixed vegetables, raw or frozen
3 1/2 ounces vermicelli

PREPARATION

In a large stockpot, add chicken to broth and bring to a boil.
Add remaining ingredients.
Cover pan and cook over low heat for 20 more minutes.

Serve hot.

Tip: If the chicken was not previously prepared, start by boiling 1 pound chicken breast (p.13).
If chicken broth is not available, use 2 fat-free chicken broth cubes in 6 cups of water and remove salt from recipe.
You can add any kind of vegetables.

NUTRITIONAL VALUE PER SERVING

Energy (Cal)	270
Cholesterol (mg)	80
Fat (g)	5
Carbohydrate (g)	32
Protein (g)	25
Fiber (g)	1

Rich in vitamins A, B3, B6, and C.
Contains carotenoids (pp.126–133).

Vegetarian

Lebanese vegetarian dishes are based on vegetables and legumes such as beans, chickpeas, and lentils.

Legumes are a vital source of vitamins (especially B1, B2, B3, and B6) and folate (pp.126–133). They are a rich source of minerals such as iron and magnesium. Legumes are nutritious, tasty, and an inexpensive protein source. They are also cholesterol free and among the best fiber sources.

Besides being healthy and delicious, legumes fill you up and help curb your appetite for higher-fat foods.

If cooked using the method described in this book, these dishes will be low in fat and rich in fiber, phytochemicals, and many nutrients, and therefore will offer many health benefits, including a lower risk of heart disease and certain types of cancer.

For more information on the nutritional value of vegetables, see page 15.

KIDNEY BEANS IN TOMATO SAUCE fassolia be zeit

serves **6** | preparation time **10 min** | cooking time **30 min**

INGREDIENTS

1 tablespoon vegetable oil
2 medium onions, finely chopped
2 garlic cloves, crushed (p.11)

4 tablespoons tomato paste
4 cups water
1 teaspoon salt
1 pinch white pepper

5 cups cooked kidney beans (p.12)

PREPARATION

In a large pot, heat oil, add onions, and stir-fry until lightly browned.
Add garlic and stir-fry for 2 more minutes.

Dissolve tomato paste in water, then add to onions and garlic mixture.
Add salt and white pepper. Bring to a boil.

Add kidney beans. Mix and bring to a boil. Cook over low heat for 20 minutes or until mixture thickens.

Serve hot or cold.

Tip: You can add one serving Cilantro and Garlic (p.10) to the onion mixture and continue the preparation.
If kidney beans were uncooked, start by boiling 2 cups of dried kidney beans (p.12).

NUTRITIONAL VALUE PER SERVING

Energy (Cal)	330
Cholesterol (mg)	0
Fat (g)	3
Carbohydrate (g)	57
Protein (g)	18
Fiber (g)	15

Rich in fiber, folate, magnesium, potassium, and vitamins B1 and B6.
Contains lycopene and isoflavone (pp.126–133).

HUMMUS BE TAHINI
chickpea dip | serves 5 | preparation time 5 min | cooking time 15 min

INGREDIENTS

1 cup water
2 1/2 cups cooked chickpeas (p.12)

4 garlic cloves, crushed (p.11)
1 teaspoon salt
3 tablespoons tahini
2 tablespoons fat-free plain yogurt
1/2 cup lemon juice

1 pinch cumin
4 tablespoons olive oil
1/4 bunch parsley leaves, finely chopped

Tip: If chickpeas were uncooked, start by boiling 1 cup dried chickpeas (p.12), or use canned chickpeas.

PREPARATION

In a large pot, bring water to a boil.
Add chickpeas; cook over low heat until tender.
Drain and set aside cooking liquid.
Mash chickpeas using a food processor, adding cooking liquid if necessary.

In a separate bowl, mix garlic, salt, tahini, yogurt and lemon juice.
Add to mashed chickpeas. Mix well to obtain a soft, creamy consistency.

Put in a serving dish, and garnish with cumin, olive oil and chopped parsley.

Serve cold.

BABA GHANNUJ eggplant dip
serves 3 | preparation time 15 min | cooking time 15 min

INGREDIENTS

1 large eggplant

2 garlic cloves, crushed (p.11)
1 teaspoon salt
2 tablespoons tahini
1 tablespoon fat-free plain yogurt
4 tablespoons lemon juice

2 tablespoons olive oil
1 pinch parsley leaves, finely chopped

PREPARATION

Peel eggplant; wrap it with plastic wrap.
Cook in microwave for 10 minutes.
Unwrap and mash with a fork, allow to cool.

In a separate bowl, mix garlic, salt, tahini, yogurt, and lemon juice.
Add to mashed eggplant and mix again.

Put in a serving dish. Garnish with olive oil and chopped parsley.

Serve cold.

Note: To prepare Zucchini Dip, substitute eggplant with pulp of 5 medium zucchinis, boiled and drained.

Hummus Be Tahini chickpea dip

NUTRITIONAL VALUE PER SERVING

Energy (Cal)	330
Cholesterol (mg)	0
Fat (g)	18
Carbohydrate (g)	32
Protein (g)	10
Fiber (g)	8

Rich in folate and vitamins B6, C, and K.
Contains isoflavone (pp.126–133).

Baba Ghannuj eggplant dip

NUTRITIONAL VALUE PER SERVING

Energy (Cal)	205
Cholesterol (mg)	0
Fat (g)	14
Carbohydrate (g)	16
Protein (g)	4
Fiber (g)	2

Rich in vitamins A and C (pp.126–133).

Energy (Cal)	500
Cholesterol (mg)	4
Fat (g)	7
Carbohydrate (g)	80
Protein (g)	30
Fiber (g)	12

Rich in calcium, fiber, folate, magnesium, phosphorus, and vitamins B2 and B6. Contains allylic sulfite and isoflavone (pp.126–133).

FATTET HUMMUS
chickpeas with yogurt

serves **5** | preparation time **10 min** | cooking time **20 min**

INGREDIENTS

2 cups water
1 teaspoon salt
1 teaspoon cumin
5 garlic cloves, crushed (p.11)
5 cups cooked chickpeas (p.12)

4 cups fat-free plain yogurt
1 teaspoon dried mint
1/2 teaspoon tahini

1 medium loaf pita bread, toasted
5 teaspoons pine nuts, toasted (p.13)

PREPARATION

In a large pot, bring water to a boil.
Add 1/2 of the salt, cumin, garlic, plus all the chickpeas. Cook over medium heat until tender.
Set aside.

In a separate bowl, mix yogurt, mint, and tahini. Add remaining garlic and salt.
Mix again and set aside.

Cut bread into small squares.
Put hot chickpeas with some of their cooking liquid in a serving dish. Add bread and cover with yogurt.
Garnish with pine nuts and remaining cumin.

Tip: If chickpeas were uncooked, start by boiling 2 cups dried chickpeas (p.12), or use canned chickpeas.

NUTRITIONAL VALUE PER SERVING

Rich in folate and vitamins B6, C, and K. Contains lycopene (pp.126–133).

Energy (Cal)	260
Cholesterol (mg)	0
Fat (g)	6
Carbohydrate (g)	42
Protein (g)	10
Fiber (g)	9

MOUSSAKA

serves **4** | preparation time **10 min** | cooking time **60 min**

INGREDIENTS

1 large eggplant, unpeeled
4 cups water
1 tablespoon sea salt
Vegetable oil

1 tablespoon vegetable oil
2 small onions, thinly sliced
5 garlic cloves, finely chopped
1 14.5-ounce can diced tomatoes
1 teaspoon salt
1/4 teaspoon allspice
2 cups cooked chickpeas (p.12)
2 cups water

PREPARATION

Cut eggplant into 10 pieces, each 3/4 inch thick.
Soak in water and sea salt for 10 minutes.
Drain well and put in a baking dish lightly greased with oil in preheated oven (475°) for 30 minutes.
Flip from time to time.

In a large pot, heat oil, add onions, garlic, and stir-fry until lightly browned.
Add tomatoes and seasonings; stir-fry for 2 more minutes. Add chickpeas and water.
Cook over high heat and bring to a boil.
Add chickpea mixture to eggplant; cover with aluminum foil.
Cook over low heat for 30 more minutes or until mixture thickens.

Serve cold.

Tip: It is better to keep the eggplant unpeeled, since its skin is very rich in fiber, vitamins, and minerals.
Instead of 1 can diced tomatoes, you can chop 4 fresh medium tomatoes.
If chickpeas were uncooked, start by boiling 3/4 cup of dried chickpeas (p.12), or use canned chickpeas.

NUTRITIONAL VALUE PER SERVING

Energy (Cal)	330
Cholesterol (mg)	0
Fat (g)	8
Carbohydrate (g)	52
Protein (g)	12
Fiber (g)	15

Rich in fiber, folate, and vitamins B6 and K.
Contains allylic sulfite and tannins (pp.126–133).

MOUDARDARA lentils with rice

serves **4** | preparation time **5 min** | cooking time **45 min**

INGREDIENTS

2 tablespoons vegetable oil
3 small onions, thinly sliced

2 cups water
1 teaspoon salt
1/2 teaspoon black pepper
1/2 cup short-grain rice, soaked in water
        for 1/2 hour

2 cups cooked lentils (p.12)

Tip: If lentils were uncooked, start by boiling 3/4 cup of lentils.
Serve with green salad and lemon dressing that is rich in vitamin C to enhance the absorption of iron in lentils.

PREPARATION

In a large pot, heat oil, add onions, and stir-fry for 10 minutes until fully brown and crispy. Remove 1/2 the onions and set aside for later use.

Add water and seasonings to the remaining onions in the pot.
Drain rice, then add to pot and bring to boil.
Cover and cook over low heat for 10 minutes.

Add lentils and slowly stir the mixture.
Bring to a boil again, cover, and cook over very low heat without stirring for 20 minutes or until all water evaporates.

In a serving plate, garnish with remaining onions.
Serve hot or cold.

Energy (Cal)	250
Cholesterol (mg)	0
Fat (g)	4
Carbohydrate (g)	47
Protein (g)	7
Fiber (g)	13

Rich in folate and vitamins B6, C, and E.
Contains carotene (pp.126–133).

MEHSHI KATEI
meatless stuffed vegetables

serves 5 | preparation time 30 min | cooking time 60 min

INGREDIENTS

2 pounds small eggplants
2 pounds small zucchinis
7 ounces small green bell peppers

Stuffing
1/2 cup short-grain rice
2 medium onions, finely chopped
1 bunch parsley leaves, finely chopped
1 14.5-ounce can diced tomatoes
1 pinch dried mint
1 teaspoon allspice
1 teaspoon salt
1 pinch white pepper
1/2 cup lemon juice
1 tablespoon olive oil

7/8 cup tomato sauce
1 cup water

PREPARATION

Remove the pulp of the zucchinis, and carve
out the insides of the eggplants and green
peppers.

In a large bowl, drain rice and mix with
remaining stuffing ingredients.
Stuff vegetables to 3/4 full and arrange
horizontally in a deep pot.

Mix tomato sauce with water and pour over
vegetables.
Place a heavy plate on vegetables to keep
them in place; add more water to cover the
plate.
Bring to boil.
Cover pot and cook over low heat for 1 hour
or until rice is tender.

Serve hot or cold.

Tip: Instead of 1 can diced tomatoes, you can chop 4 fresh medium tomatoes.

NUTRITIONAL VALUE PER SERVING

Energy (Cal)	190
Cholesterol (mg)	0
Fat (g)	4
Carbohydrate (g)	32
Protein (g)	6
Fiber (g)	7

Rich in vitamins B6, C, K, and E.
Contains isoflavone and lycopene
(pp.126–133).

GREEN BEANS IN TOMATO SAUCE loubieh be zeit

serves **4** | preparation time **25 min** | cooking time **45 min**

INGREDIENTS

1 tablespoon vegetable oil
1 large onion, finely chopped
10 garlic cloves, finely diced
2 pounds frozen green beans
1 14.5-ounce can diced tomatoes

1 tablespoon tomato paste
1 1/2 cups water
1 teaspoon salt
1/4 teaspoon allspice

Tip: You can use 3 pounds fresh green beans, cut
into 2-inch pieces.
Instead of 1 can diced tomatoes, you can chop 4
fresh medium tomatoes.

PREPARATION

In a large pot, heat oil, add onions and
stir-fry until lightly browned.
Add garlic and stir-fry for 2 more minutes.
Add green beans and stir-fry for 20 minutes or
until very tender.
Add tomatoes and stir-fry for 2 more minutes.

Dissolve tomato paste in water.
Add to green beans, plus seasonings.
Cook over high heat and bring to a boil.
Cover pan; cook over low heat for 20 more
minutes (add water and use pressure cooker
if needed).

Serve cold with onions.

*Note: To prepare Green Bean Stew, add 1/2
pound Cooked Cubed Beef (p.8) and 1/2 cup
water and serve with Cooked Rice (p.72).
To prepare Zucchini in Tomato Sauce, substitute
green beans with pulp of 5 medium zucchinis,
boiled and drained.*

NUTRITIONAL VALUE PER SERVING

Energy (Cal)	280
Cholesterol (mg)	0
Fat (g)	5
Carbohydrate (g)	45
Protein (g)	14
Fiber (g)	13

Rich in folate and vitamin K.
Contains indoles (pp.126–133).

MOUJADARA mashed lentils

serves 3 | preparation time 15 min | cooking time 40 min

INGREDIENTS

1 tablespoon vegetable oil
1 medium onion, finely chopped
1/4 cup short-grain rice, soaked in water
        for 1/2 hour

2 cups water
2 cups cooked lentils (p.12)
1/2 teaspoon allspice
1 teaspoon salt

Tip: If lentils were uncooked, start by boiling 3/4 cup
lentils.
It is preferable to mash lentils with their skin, which is
rich in fiber, vitamins and minerals.

PREPARATION

In a large pot, heat oil, add onions and
stir-fry until lightly browned.
Add drained rice and 1 cup of the water.
Bring to a boil. Cover and cook over low
heat for 10 minutes.

Meanwhile, in a large pot, bring remaining
water to a boil.
Add lentils; cook over medium heat until
tender.
Mash the mixture in a food processor. Add
to rice with seasonings.

Cook over low heat, stirring constantly.
Remove from heat as soon as boiling starts.
Pour immediately into the serving plate,
allow to cool, and serve cold with fresh
vegetables and salad.

NUTRITIONAL VALUE PER SERVING

Energy (Cal)	290
Cholesterol (mg)	0
Fat (g)	6
Carbohydrate (g)	51
Protein (g)	8
Fiber (g)	11

Rich in fiber, magnesium, and vitamins
B6 and C.
Contains lycopene (pp.126–133).

BULGUR WITH TOMATO

serves **3** | preparation time **10 min** | cooking time **40 min**

INGREDIENTS

1 tablespoon vegetable oil
1 large onion, finely chopped
2 garlic cloves, crushed (p.11)
1 14.5-ounce can diced tomatoes

1 cup coarse bulgur
1 1/2 cups water
1/4 teaspoon allspice
1 teaspoon salt

PREPARATION

In a large pot, heat oil, add onions, and
stir-fry until lightly browned.
Add garlic and stir-fry for 2 more minutes.
Add tomatoes and stir-fry for 3 more
minutes.

Add remaining ingredients and stir.
Bring to a boil.
Cover pot and cook over very low heat for 25
more minutes or until water evaporates.

Serve with plain yogurt.

Tip: Instead of 1 can diced tomatoes, you can chop 4 fresh medium tomatoes.

NUTRITIONAL VALUE PER SERVING

Energy (Cal)	145
Cholesterol (mg)	0
Fat (g)	9
Carbohydrate (g)	13
Protein (g)	3
Fiber (g)	11

Rich in fiber, folate, potassium, pantothenic acid, and vitamins A, C, and K.
Contains carotenoids (pp.126–133).

STIR-FRIED CHICORY WITH ONIONS hendbeh be zeit

serves **5** | preparation time **30 min** | cooking time **15 min**

INGREDIENTS

2 tablespoons vegetable oil
2 large onions, thinly sliced

2 garlic cloves, crushed (p.11)
2 large heads boiled chicory, finely
        shredded
1 teaspoon salt
4 tablespoons lemon juice

1 lemon, sliced in rounds

PREPARATION

In a large pan, heat oil, add onions, and
stir-fry until fully brown and crispy.
Remove and put on paper towels to dry. Set
aside for later use.

In the same pan, add garlic and stir-fry for
1 minute.
Add chicory and stir-fry for 5 more minutes.
Add salt and lemon juice, and stir-fry for a
few more minutes.

Garnish with onions and lemon slices.

Serve cold.

WHITE SPAGHETTI

serves **6** | preparation time **10 min** | cooking time **30 min**

INGREDIENTS

1 pound spaghetti

White Sauce
5 cups water
10 tablespoons nonfat dry milk
1/4 nutmeg, grated, or 1/4 teaspoon ground
        nutmeg
1 teaspoon salt
1/2 teaspoon white pepper
4 tablespoons cornstarch

1/2 cup mozzarella cheese, grated

PREPARATION

Cook spaghetti in boiling water. Drain well.

In a separate pot, mix white sauce
ingredients and cook over low heat.
Stir constantly until mixture starts to thicken.

Add spaghetti and grated cheese to white
sauce.
Cook over low heat for 2 more minutes,
stirring constantly.

Serve hot.

Tip: You can replace 5 cups water and 10 tablespoons nonfat dry milk with 3 cups fresh skim milk and 2 cups water.
You can add 1 egg to white sauce mixture.

NUTRITIONAL VALUE PER SERVING

Energy (Cal)	420
Cholesterol (mg)	30
Fat (g)	6
Carbohydrate (g)	72
Protein (g)	20
Fiber (g)	2

Rich in calcium, protein, and vitamin B3 (pp.126–133).

OVEN-BAKED OMELET

serves **4** | preparation time **15 min** | cooking time **30 min**

INGREDIENTS

1 small onion, finely chopped
1 teaspoon salt
1/2 teaspoon allspice
1/4 teaspoon black pepper
1/2 bunch parsley leaves, finely chopped
1 zucchini, grated
1/4 green bell pepper, finely chopped

6 eggs
1/2 teaspoon red-wine or grape vinegar
1/4 cup water
4 tablespoons all-purpose flour
1/2 teaspoon baking powder
1 tablespoon nonfat dry milk

Vegetable oil
4 tablespoons dried bread crumbs
4 tablespoons mozzarella cheese, grated

PREPARATION

Mix salt, allspice, and black pepper. Rub onion in spices, coating thoroughly.
Add vegetables and parsley and mix again.

In a separate bowl, mix eggs with vinegar and water.
Add flour, baking powder, and dry milk. Mix well.
Pour over vegetables and mix again.

Grease a 13x9-inch baking dish with oil.
Sprinkle dried bread crumbs on pan.
Pour egg mixture in and sprinkle cheese on top.
Bake in a preheated oven (475°) for 20 minutes or until top is golden brown.

Serve hot with Fattoush (p.18) or Tabbouleh (p.16).

Tip: You can replace 1/4 cup water and 1 tablespoon nonfat dry milk with 1/4 cup fresh skim milk.

NUTRITIONAL VALUE PER SERVING

Energy (Cal)	280
Cholesterol (mg)	330
Fat (g)	11
Carbohydrate (g)	27
Protein (g)	18
Fiber (g)	3

Rich in protein and vitamins A, B12, and D.

Beef Platters

Lebanese dishes are based on moderate amounts of meat, with the focus on grain products, legumes, and vegetables. They are typically low in fat and high in fiber, which is consistent with the international dietary guidelines for healthy eating. In this chapter, the dishes are prepared with beef. Except for the Roast Beef recipe (p.68), you may replace beef with lamb or goat meat.

Meat, in general, is highly nutritious, rich in zinc and vitamins B3, B6, B12 (pp.126–133). It is an excellent source of heme-iron (pp.126–133) that helps prevent anemia and enhance the immune system. Meat supplies complete proteins, essential to make new body proteins, cells, and muscles, and to ensure healthy growth.

Meat also contains, depending on its source, saturated fats and cholesterol. Choose lean cuts such as beef sirloin and fillet. Trim the fat before use. Broil, roast, or grill; this way you won't add fat during cooking. Sauté, stir-fry, or broil using vegetable oils low in saturated fats such as corn, sunflower, soy, or canola, rather than butter and ghee.

BURGHOL BE DFIN
bulgur with meat and chickpeas

serves **5** | preparation time **5 min** | cooking time **30 min**

INGREDIENTS

1 tablespoon vegetable oil
10 pearl onions

1/2 pound Cooked Cubed Beef (p.8)
2 cups cooked chickpeas (p.12)
2 cups coarse bulgur
3 cups water
1 teaspoon salt
1/2 teaspoon ground cinnamon
1/2 teaspoon allspice
1/2 teaspoon caraway powder

PREPARATION

In a large pot, heat oil, add onions, and stir-fry until lightly browned. Onions should remain whole.

Add remaining ingredients and mix well. Bring to a boil. Mix again and then cover. Cook over low heat for 25 minutes.

Serve hot with fat-free yogurt.

Tip: If you don't have pearl onions, cut 2 medium onions in quarters.
If the meat was not previously prepared, start by cooking 1/2 pound cubed beef (p.8).
If chickpeas were uncooked, start by cooking 3/4 cup dried chickpeas (p.12), or use canned chickpeas.

NUTRITIONAL VALUE PER SERVING

Energy (Cal)	445
Cholesterol (mg)	22
Fat (g)	8
Carbohydrate (g)	67
Protein (g)	26
Fiber (g)	16

Rich in fiber, folate, magnesium, protein, and vitamins B3, B6, and B12.
Contains isoflavone (pp.126–133).

NUTRITIONAL VALUE PER SERVING

Rich in zinc and vitamins B3, B6, B12, C, and K (pp.126–133).

Energy (Cal)	510
Cholesterol (mg)	96
Fat (g)	29
Carbohydrate (g)	14
Protein (g)	48
Fiber (g)	3

SHAWARMA
sirloin steak strips with tahini sauce

serves 5 | preparation time 10 min | soaking time 6 hrs | cooking time 50 min

INGREDIENTS

2 pounds sirloin beef steak, cut into strips
3 tablespoons vegetable oil
4 tablespoons red-wine or grape vinegar
1 teaspoon salt
1/4 teaspoon black pepper
1/4 teaspoon allspice
1/4 teaspoon ground cinnamon
1/4 teaspoon cardamom, crushed
1/4 teaspoon mastic, crushed
1/4 nutmeg, grated, or 1/4 teaspoon ground
    nutmeg

Tahini Sauce
5 tablespoons tahini
1/2 teaspoon salt
1/2 cup water
2 garlic cloves, crushed (p.11)
5 tablespoons lemon juice

Garnishes
2 onions, thinly sliced
2 teaspoons sumac
2 tomatoes, finely diced
1/2 bunch parsley leaves, finely chopped

Tip: Marinate large amounts of meat, divide and freeze for 2 months.

PREPARATION

Mix steak strips with seasonings, then marinate
for 6 hours, stirring every 1 hour.
Put on a large rimmed baking sheet; cover with
aluminum foil.
Cook in preheated oven (475°) for 40 minutes.

Mix tahini sauce ingredients in a food processor.
Set aside.

Scrub onions with sumac until they are
thoroughly coated.
Pour tahini sauce over hot meat.
Serve with onions, tomatoes, and parsley.

NUTRITIONAL VALUE PER SERVING

Rich in complete proteins, zinc, and vitamins B3 and B12 (pp.126–133).

Energy (Cal)	280
Cholesterol (mg)	185
Fat (g)	18
Carbohydrate (g)	6
Protein (g)	23
Fiber (g)	1

MEATLOAF WITH EGGS

serves 5 | preparation time 20 min | cooking time 40 min

INGREDIENTS

1 pound lean ground beef
3 garlic cloves, crushed (p.11)
1 teaspoon salt
1/2 teaspoon allspice
1/2 teaspoon white pepper
1 pinch red pepper
3 tablespoons dried bread crumbs

3 eggs, hard-boiled
Corn oil

1 tablespoon cornstarch
1/4 cup water

PREPARATION

Blend ground beef in a food processor on high speed until it becomes like a dough (add water if needed).
In a medium bowl, mix ground beef with garlic, seasonings, and dried bread crumbs. Knead with hands until it becomes a dough. Roll dough with a wooden rolling pin into a 12x10-inch piece.

Arrange eggs in the middle of the beef. Fold beef over eggs and tightly seal the edges with wet fingertips.
In a nonstick pan lightly greased with oil, brown meatloaf, turning occasionally.
Cover with water. Bring to a boil.
Cover pan and cook over low heat for 30 minutes or until meat is no longer pink inside.
Remove meatloaf from water.
Reserve the broth for later use.
Cut meatloaf into 15 equal slices.

Dissolve cornstarch in water.
Add to 1 cup of broth, stir constantly over low heat until sauce thickens.

Serve hot with sauce and roasted potatoes.

ROAST BEEF

serves 5 | preparation time 20 min | cooking time 90 min

INGREDIENTS

2 pounds roast beef
7 garlic cloves, cut in half
1 tablespoon pistachios

1 tablespoon vegetable oil
2 medium onions, thinly sliced
2 garlic cloves, crushed (p.11)
1 cup sliced carrots
1 medium potato, diced

1 1/2 quarts water
1 Bouquet (p.8)
1 teaspoon salt
1/2 teaspoon allspice
2 tablespoons lemon juice
1 large apple, diced

1 tablespoon cornstarch

Tip: Prepare large amounts of roast beef and freeze for later use. Freeze the sauce separately.

PREPARATION

Using a sharp knife, pierce roast beef. Insert garlic and pistachios.

In a heavy pot or Dutch oven lightly greased with oil, brown meat, turning occasionally. Remove from pot and set aside.
In the same pot, add onions, cook until translucent, then add other vegetables, stirring constantly until tender.

Return roast beef to pot and cover with water. Wrap and tie contents of Bouquet in cheesecloth; add to pot. Add remaining ingredients (except cornstarch) and bring to a boil. Cover pan and cook over low heat for 1 1/2 hours (40 minutes in a pressure cooker). Remove roast beef, allow to cool, and cut into 10 equal slices.

To make the sauce, remove Bouquet from the pot, add cornstarch to the remaining vegetables and liquid, and blend in a food processor. Return liquid to pot, and stir constantly over low heat for 2 minutes.

Add sauce to roast beef.
Serve hot with Mashed Potatoes (p.70).

Roast Beef

NUTRITIONAL VALUE PER SERVING

Energy (Cal)	470
Cholesterol (mg)	103
Fat (g)	19
Carbohydrate (g)	29
Protein (g)	46
Fiber (g)	4

Rich in zinc and vitamins A, B3, B6, and B12.
Contains B-carotene (pp.126–133).

Mashed Potatoes

NUTRITIONAL VALUE PER SERVING

Energy (Cal)	200
Cholesterol (mg)	0
Fat (g)	0
Carbohydrate (g)	43
Protein (g)	7
Fiber (g)	3

Rich in vitamins B6 and C (pp.126–133).

MASHED POTATOES

serves **4** | preparation time **10 min** | cooking time **30 min**

INGREDIENTS

3 tablespoons nonfat dry milk
1 cup water
1 pinch nutmeg
1/4 teaspoon white pepper
1 teaspoon salt
6 medium potatoes, boiled and mashed

Tip: Instead of 1 cup water and 3 tablespoons nonfat
dry milk, you can use 1 cup fresh skim milk.
Potatoes are more nutritious if kept unpeeled
because their skin is very rich in fiber, vitamins, and
minerals.

PREPARATION

In a small bowl, mix dry milk, water, and
seasonings.
Add to mashed potatoes in a large pot.
Stir mixture over low heat to obtain a soft,
creamy consistency.

Serve hot with Roast Beef (p.68).

ARTICHOKE STEW

serves **4** | preparation time **5 min** | cooking time **30 min**

INGREDIENTS

1 tablespoon vegetable oil
1 large onion, finely chopped
2 garlic cloves, crushed (p.11)

1/2 pound Cooked Cubed Beef (p.8)
1 pound frozen artichoke
1 1/2 cups water
1 serving Cilantro and Garlic (p.10)
4 tablespoons lemon juice
1 teaspoon salt
1/4 teaspoon allspice

PREPARATION

In a large pot, heat oil, add onions and
stir-fry until lightly browned.
Add garlic and stir-fry for 2 more minutes.

Add remaining ingredients. Bring to a boil.
Cover pot; cook over low heat for 20 more
minutes or until mixture thickens.

Serve hot with Cooked Rice (p.72).

*Note: To prepare Cauliflower Stew, substitute
artichoke with 2 pounds frozen cauliflower.*

Tip: If the meat was not previously prepared, start by cooking 1/2 pound raw cubed beef (p.8).

COOKED RICE

INGREDIENTS

2 cups long-grain rice
2 tablespoons vermicelli (if desired)
1 teaspoon salt
4 cups water

Tip: You can use 1 teaspoon oil to stir-fry vermicelli. If you do not use vermicelli, start preparation by stir-frying the rice.

PREPARATION

Wash rice and drain.
In a saucepan, preferably nonstick, stir-fry vermicelli until lightly browned.
Add rice and salt, then stir-fry for 2 more minutes.
Add water and mix well. Bring to a boil. Stir again.
Cover pan. Cook without stirring over very low heat for 25 minutes.

Artichoke Stew

NUTRITIONAL VALUE PER SERVING

Energy (Cal)	210
Cholesterol (mg)	27
Fat (g)	7
Carbohydrate (g)	17
Protein (g)	20
Fiber (g)	7

Rich in fiber, folate, and vitamins B6, B12, and C.
Contains indoles (pp.126–133).

Cooked Rice

NUTRITIONAL VALUE PER SERVING
(without vermicelli)

Energy (Cal)	240
Cholesterol (mg)	0
Fat (g)	0
Carbohydrate (g)	55
Protein (g)	5
Fiber (g)	1

Rich in vitamins B6, C, K, and E.
Contains isoflavone and lycopene (pp.126–133).

Energy (Cal)	215
Cholesterol (mg)	27
Fat (g)	7
Carbohydrate (g)	19
Protein (g)	19
Fiber (g)	4

Rich in folate and vitamins B3, B6, B12, C, and K.
Contains carotenoids and lycopene (pp.126–133).

OKRA STEW

serves **4** | preparation time **10 min** | cooking time **30 min**

INGREDIENTS

1 tablespoon vegetable oil
1 medium onion, finely chopped
2 garlic cloves, crushed (p.11)

10 ounces okra, canned or frozen
1 14.5-ounce can diced tomatoes

1/2 pound Cooked Cubed Beef (p.8)
1 1/2 cups water
1 serving Cilantro and Garlic (p.10)
1 teaspoon salt
2 tablespoons lemon juice

PREPARATION

In a large pot, heat oil, add onions and stir-fry until lightly browned.
Add garlic and stir-fry for 2 more minutes.

Add okra; stir-fry slowly for 5 minutes.
Add tomatoes and cook for 2 more minutes.

Add remaining ingredients. Bring to a boil. Cover pot. Cook over low heat for 30 minutes or until mixture thickens.

Serve hot with Cooked Rice (p.72).

Tip: Instead of 1 can diced tomatoes, you can chop 4 fresh medium tomatoes.
If the meat was not previously prepared, start by cooking 1/2 pound of raw cubed beef (p.8).

NUTRITIONAL VALUE PER SERVING

Energy (Cal)	225
Cholesterol (mg)	26
Fat (g)	6
Carbohydrate (g)	19
Protein (g)	23
Fiber (g)	1

Rich in calcium and vitamins B6 and B12
(pp.126–133).

LABAN EMMO
yogurt soup with cubed beef

serves **5** | preparation time **10 min** | cooking time **15 min**

INGREDIENTS

1 tablespoon vegetable oil
10 pearl onions
5 garlic cloves, crushed (p.11)
1/2 pound Cooked Cubed Beef (p.8)
1 cup water

Labanyieh (Yogurt Soup)
4 cups fat-free plain yogurt
1 tablespoon cornstarch
1 teaspoon tahini
1/2 teaspoon salt
1 pinch white pepper

1 teaspoon dried mint

PREPARATION

In a large pot, heat oil, add onions, and stir-fry until lightly browned. Onions should remain whole.
Add garlic and stir-fry for 2 minutes.
Add beef and water; cook over low heat for 10 more minutes.

In a separate bowl, mix yogurt soup ingredients.
Add to beef gradually, stirring constantly.
Bring to a boil.

Sprinkle mint over top.
Serve hot with Cooked Rice (p.72).

Tip: If you don't have pearl onions, replace with 2 medium onions cut into quarters.
If the meat was not previously prepared, start by cooking 1/2 pound raw cubed beef (p.8).

GREEN PEA STEW

serves **4** | preparation time **5 min** | cooking time **30 min**

INGREDIENTS

1 tablespoon vegetable oil
2 medium onions, finely chopped
2 garlic cloves, crushed (p.11)
1 14.5-ounce can diced tomatoes

1/2 pound Cooked Cubed Beef (p.8)
2 cups canned or frozen peas and carrots
2 cups water
1 teaspoon salt
1 pinch cinnamon
1 pinch allspice

PREPARATION

In a large pot, heat oil, add onions and
stir-fry until lightly browned.
Add garlic and stir-fry for 2 minutes.
Add tomatoes and stir for 3 more minutes.

Stir in remaining ingredients.
Bring to a boil.
Stir again, cover pot, and cook over low heat
for 30 minutes or until mixture thickens.

Serve hot with Cooked Rice (p.72).

Tip: Instead of 1 can diced tomatoes, you can chop 4 fresh medium tomatoes.
If the meat was not previously prepared, start by cooking 1/2 pound raw cubed beef (p.8).

NUTRITIONAL VALUE PER SERVING

Energy (Cal)	260
Cholesterol (mg)	27
Fat (g)	8
Carbohydrate (g)	26
Protein (g)	21
Fiber (g)	5

Rich in vitamins A, B6, B12, C, and K.
Contains carotene and isoflavone (pp.126–133).

KIDNEY BEAN STEW

serves **6** | preparation time **10 min** | cooking time **30 min**

INGREDIENTS

1 tablespoon vegetable oil
1 large onion, finely chopped
2 garlic cloves, crushed (p.11)
1 14.5-ounce can diced tomatoes

1/2 pound Cooked Cubed Beef (p.8)
5 cups cooked kidney beans (p.12)
2 cups water
1 teaspoon salt
1 pinch white pepper

PREPARATION

In a large pot, heat oil, add onions, and stir-fry until lightly browned.
Add garlic and stir-fry for 2 minutes.
Add tomatoes and stir-fry over high heat for 3 more minutes.

Add remaining ingredients. Bring to a boil. Cover pot and cook over low heat for 20 more minutes or until mixture thickens.

Serve hot with Cooked Rice (p.72).

Tip: Instead of 1 can diced tomatoes, you can chop 4 fresh medium tomatoes.
If the meat was not previously prepared, start by cooking 1/2 pound raw cubed beef (p.8).
If kidney beans were uncooked, start by boiling 2 cups dried kidney beans (p.12), or use canned kidney beans.

NUTRITIONAL VALUE PER SERVING

Energy (Cal)	350
Cholesterol (mg)	18
Fat (g)	5
Carbohydrate (g)	49
Protein (g)	27
Fiber (g)	14

Rich in fiber, folate, iron, magnesium, potassium and vitamins B6 and B12.
Contains isoflavone and lycopene (pp.126–133).

Energy (Cal)	195
Cholesterol (mg)	18
Fat (g)	2
Carbohydrate (g)	32
Protein (g)	12
Fiber (g)	5

Rich in vitamins B6, B12, C, and E.
Contains B-carotene (pp.126–133).

STUFFED ZUCCHINIS

serves 5 | preparation time 30 min | cooking time 60 min

INGREDIENTS

5 medium zucchinis

Stuffing
1/2 cup short-grain rice, soaked in water
    for 1/2 hour
1 tomato, finely chopped
1 serving Cooked Ground Beef (p.9)
1/4 teaspoon allspice
1/4 teaspoon cinnamon
1 teaspoon salt

7/8 cup tomato sauce
3 cups water
6 tablespoons lemon juice
1 teaspoon dried mint
3 garlic cloves, crushed (p.11)

Tip: You can use 5 1/4 ounces raw ground beef.

PREPARATION

Cut zucchinis in half crosswise. Scoop out the pulp and keep it for later use (refer to note p.42, 51, or 82).

Drain rice and mix with the remaining stuffing ingredients.
Stuff each zucchini to 3/4 full and arrange standing up vertically in a deep pot.

In a separate bowl, mix rest of ingredients. Pour over zucchinis.
Place a heavy plate on zucchinis to keep them in place; add more water to cover the plate.
Bring to a boil.
Cover pan and cook over low heat for 1 hour or until rice is tender.

Serve hot with plain yogurt.

Note: To prepare Stuffed Eggplants, substitute zucchinis with eggplants.

NUTRITIONAL VALUE PER SERVING

Energy (Cal)	390
Cholesterol (mg)	60
Fat (g)	12
Carbohydrate (g)	45
Protein (g)	29
Fiber (g)	11

Rich in calcium, fiber, magnesium, zinc, and vitamins B3, B6, and B12 (pp.126–133).

Energy (Cal)	230
Cholesterol (mg)	290
Fat (g)	12
Carbohydrate (g)	8
Protein (g)	22
Fiber (g)	1

Rich in folate and vitamins B2, B6, B12, C, and K.
Contains B-carotene (pp.126–133).

ZUCCHINI OMELET

serves 5 | preparation time 5 min | soaking time 30 min | cooking time 30 min

INGREDIENTS

Pulp of 5 medium zucchinis (without skins;
      see p.80)
2 teaspoons salt

6 eggs
1 serving Cooked Ground Beef (p.9)
1 medium tomato, finely chopped
2 garlic cloves, crushed (p.11)
1 tablespoon all-purpose flour
1 pinch white pepper
1 pinch red pepper

1/2 cup mozzarella cheese, grated

PREPARATION

Add salt to zucchini pulp; mix and set aside
for 1/2 hour. Squeeze well with hands to
drain. Discard water.

Mix with remaining ingredients (except
cheese).
Place mixture in a lightly greased 13x9-inch
baking dish.
Sprinkle cheese over top.
Bake in preheated oven (475°) for 30
minutes.

Serve hot or cold with salad.

*Note: To prepare Zucchini Dip, refer to note
p.42.
To prepare Zucchini in Tomato Sauce, refer
to note p.51.*

KEBBE LABANYIEH
kebbe in yogurt soup

serves 5 | preparation time 30 min | cooking time 60 min

INGREDIENTS

Kebbe Rolls
1 small onion
1 teaspoon salt
1/2 teaspoon allspice
1 pinch marjoram
1 pinch cinnamon
1 pinch dried mint
1 pinch dried basil
7 ounces lean ground beef
1 cup fine bulgur, soaked in water
        for 1/2 hour

Stuffing
1 serving Cooked Ground Beef (p.9)
1 tablespoon pine nuts, toasted (p.13)

Labanyieh (Yogurt Soup)
1/2 cup short-grain rice, soaked in water
        for 1/2 hour
1 cup water
4 cups fat-free plain yogurt
1 teaspoon cornstarch
1 teaspoon tahini
1 serving Cilantro and Garlic (p.10)
1/2 teaspoon salt
1 pinch white pepper

PREPARATION

Mash onion with seasonings in a food processor on high speed.
Gradually add lean ground beef to onion mixture, blending continuously until mixture becomes like dough.
Knead bulgur with hands while in soaking water. Drain well and then add to meat.
Blend again until dough becomes smooth and elastic (add water if needed).

Cut kebbe dough into 25 equal rolls. Hollow out each piece, then stuff with ground beef and pine nuts. Tightly seal the edges with wet fingertips. Arrange the rolls on a rimmed baking sheet lightly greased with oil. Cook in preheated oven (475°) for 20 minutes; flip rolls every 5 minutes until lightly browned. Remove rolls and set aside.

Drain rice, then put in a deep pot. Cover with water and bring to a boil. Cover pot. Cook over low heat for 10 minutes or until rice is tender. In a separate bowl, mix remaining ingredients; add to rice, stirring constantly. Bring to a boil. Add kebbe rolls and stir for 1 more minute.

Serve hot.

Tip: Prepare, bake, and freeze large amounts of kebbe rolls for later use.
If you are short on time you can divide the kebbe dough into balls and bake without stuffing. You might find ready-made kebbe rolls in specialized supermarkets.

NUTRITIONAL VALUE PER SERVING

Rich in calcium, fiber, magnesium, zinc, and vitamins B3, B6, and B12 (pp.126–133).

Energy (Cal)	390
Cholesterol (mg)	60
Fat (g)	12
Carbohydrate (g)	45
Protein (g)	29
Fiber (g)	11

KEBBE IN A PAN

serves 8 | preparation time 30 min | cooking time 50 min

INGREDIENTS

Kebbe Dough
1 medium onion
2 teaspoons salt
1 teaspoon allspice
1/2 teaspoon marjoram
1/2 teaspoon ground cinnamon
1/2 teaspoon dried mint
1/2 teaspoon dried basil
1 pound lean ground beef
3 cups fine bulgur, soaked in water
      for 1/2 hour

Stuffing
2 servings Cooked Ground Beef (p.9)
3 tablespoons pine nuts, toasted (p.13)

2 tablespoons water
2 tablespoons oil
Vegetable oil

PREPARATION

To prepare kebbe dough, use ingredients on this page but follow the same method of preparation as on page 83.

Divide dough into 2 parts. Knead each part well. Lightly grease a large casserole dish with vegetable oil. Press first part of kebbe dough evenly into dish. Spread ground beef and pine nuts on top.

Cut remaining dough into balls. Flatten each ball into a round shape, and lay them over the ground beef and pine nuts until the entire surface is covered.
Use wet fingertips to smooth out any dents in the surface and patch up any holes.
Use a knife to decorate kebbe surface with square- or diamond-shaped cuts.

Mix water with oil. Spread on kebbe surface.
Wrap baking dish with aluminum foil.
Cook in preheated oven (475°) for 40 minutes.
Remove aluminum foil, and drizzle a bit more oil on kebbe.
Broil for 10 minutes.

Serve hot with salad or plain yogurt.

NUTRITIONAL VALUE PER SERVING

Energy (Cal)	370
Cholesterol (mg)	51
Fat (g)	9
Carbohydrate (g)	57
Protein (g)	16
Fiber (g)	5

Rich in potassium and vitamins B3, B6, B12,
C and K.
Contains zeaxanthin (pp.126–133).

SHEPHERD'S PIE

serves 8 | preparation time 20 min | cooking time 50 min

INGREDIENTS

2 tablespoons nonfat dry milk
1/2 cup water
1 teaspoon salt
1 pinch nutmeg
1 pinch white pepper
12 medium potatoes, boiled and mashed

1 teaspoon vegetable oil
2 servings Cooked Ground Beef (p.9)
1 tablespoon pine nuts, toasted (p.13)
1 cup canned corn

1 egg
1 pinch allspice
1/2 cup dried bread crumbs

Tip: Instead of 1/2 cup water and 2 tablespoons nonfat
dry milk, you can use 1/2 cup fresh skim milk.
Potatoes are more nutritious if kept unpeeled because
their skin is very rich in fiber, vitamins, and minerals.
If the meat was not previously prepared, start by
cooking 10 1/2 ounces raw ground beef (p.9).

PREPARATION

Mix milk with water and seasonings.
Add to potatoes; knead mixture well.
Divide into 2 equal parts.

Lightly grease a large casserole dish with oil,
then spread half the potatoes in the bottom.
Cover with meat, pine nuts, and corn.
Cut remaining potatoes into balls. Flatten
balls into circles.
Layer over stuffing until the entire surface is
covered.
Use wet fingertips to smooth the surface.

Mix egg with allspice and brush over the
potatoes, then sprinkle dried bread crumbs
on top.
Bake in preheated oven (475°) for 20
minutes.
Broil for 5 minutes until golden brown.

Serve hot.

NUTRITIONAL VALUE PER SERVING

Energy (Cal)	205
Cholesterol (mg)	36
Fat (g)	7
Carbohydrate (g)	19
Protein (g)	17
Fiber (g)	6

Rich in vitamins B6, B12, and C.
Contains lycopene (pp.126–133).

SHEIKH EL MEHSHI
meat-stuffed eggplants

serves **5** | preparation time **15 min** | cooking time **90 min**

INGREDIENTS

2 pounds eggplants

2 servings Cooked Ground Beef (p.9)
3 tablespoons pine nuts, toasted (p.13)
1 14.5-ounce can diced tomatoes

2 cups water
1 pinch white pepper
1 teaspoon salt
1 pinch dried mint

Tip: If the meat was not previously prepared, start by cooking 10 1/2 ounces raw ground beef (p.9). Instead of 1 can diced tomatoes, you can chop 4 fresh medium tomatoes.

PREPARATION

Put eggplants in a nonstick 13x9-inch baking dish in preheated oven (475°) for 1 hour.
Turn every 15 minutes for even cooking.

Cut an opening in each eggplant and fill with ground beef and pine nuts.
Put back in baking dish and cover with tomatoes.

Mix remaining ingredients; pour over eggplants and cover baking dish with aluminum foil.
Cook over low heat for 30 minutes or until mixture thickens.

Serve hot with Cooked Rice (p.72).

Note: To prepare Ablama (meat-stuffed zucchinis), substitute eggplants with zucchinis.

SPINACH STEW

serves **4** | preparation time **5 min** | cooking time **15 min**

INGREDIENTS

1 tablespoon vegetable oil
1 medium onion, finely chopped
1 serving Cooked Ground Beef (p.9)
1 serving Cilantro and Garlic (p.10)
1 teaspoon salt
1/4 teaspoon white pepper
1/4 teaspoon ground cinnamon
1/4 teaspoon black pepper
1 pound frozen chopped spinach
1 cup water
2 tablespoons pine nuts, toasted (p.13)
4 tablespoons lemon juice

PREPARATION

In a large pot, heat oil, add onions, and stir-fry until lightly browned.
Add Cooked Ground Beef, Cilantro and Garlic, and seasonings, stirring constantly.
Add spinach and water.
Stir and bring to a boil.
Add remaining ingredients.
Cover and cook over low heat for 15 more minutes or until mixture thickens.

Add more lemon juice, if desired, and salt to taste.

Serve hot with Cooked Rice (p.72).

Tip: If the meat was not previously prepared, start by cooking 5 1/2 ounces raw ground beef (p.9).

NUTRITIONAL VALUE PER SERVING

Energy (Cal)	190
Cholesterol (mg)	22
Fat (g)	9
Carbohydrate (g)	13
Protein (g)	14
Fiber (g)	6

Rich in folate and vitamins A, B6, B12, and C.
Contains carotenoids and lutein (pp.126–133).

KAFTA AND POTATOES

serves **4** | preparation time **20 min** | cooking time **40 min**

INGREDIENTS

1 pound kafta meat
1 green bell pepper, sliced in rounds
2 onions, sliced in rounds
4 potatoes, thinly sliced in rounds
3 tomatoes, sliced in rounds

1 quart water
2 tablespoons tomato paste
7/8 cup tomato sauce
1 teaspoon salt
1/2 teaspoon allspice
1 teaspoon oregano
1 teaspoon basil

Radishes, as garnish

PREPARATION

Divide kafta into patties (like hamburger). Broil for 30 minutes, 15 minutes each side. Add green pepper, onions, potatoes, and tomatoes.

In a large bowl, mix remaining ingredients. Pour over kafta; cover with aluminum foil. Cook in oven (475°) for 40 minutes or until potatoes soften.

Serve hot, garnished with radishes.

Tip: If kafta is not ready-made, mix 1 pound lean ground beef with 1/2 onion and 1/2 bunch of parsley leaves in a food processor. Add salt and pepper to taste.
Grill large amounts of kafta meat and put in freezer for 2 months for later use.
Potatoes are more nutritious if kept unpeeled because their skin is very rich in fiber, vitamins and minerals.

NUTRITIONAL VALUE PER SERVING

Energy (Cal)	380
Cholesterol (mg)	75
Fat (g)	8
Carbohydrate (g)	45
Protein (g)	32
Fiber (g)	7

Rich in potassium, zinc, and vitamins B3, B6, B12, C, and E.
Contains lycopene (pp.126–133).

NUTRITIONAL VALUE PER SERVING

Energy (Cal)	190
Cholesterol (mg)	54
Fat (g)	8
Carbohydrate (g)	9
Protein (g)	20
Fiber (g)	1

Rich in vitamins B3, B6, and B12.
Contains lycopene (pp.126–133).

DAWOOD BASHA
kafta meatballs with tomato sauce

serves **5** | preparation time **15 min** | cooking time **50 min**

INGREDIENTS

1 pound kafta meat

1 tablespoon vegetable oil
1 large onion, finely chopped
2 garlic cloves, crushed (p.11)
1 14.5-ounce can diced tomatoes

1 cup water
1/4 teaspoon allspice
1 teaspoon salt
1 pinch dried mint
1 pinch oregano

PREPARATION

Divide kafta meat into 20 small balls.
Put on a nonstick rimmed baking sheet in
preheated oven (475°) for 30 minutes.
Flip meatballs every 10 minutes for even
cooking. Remove and set aside.

In a large pot, heat oil, add onions, and
stir-fry until lightly browned.
Add garlic and stir-fry for 2 more minutes.
Add tomatoes and kafta; stir-fry for 3 more
minutes.

Add remaining ingredients. Bring to a boil.
Cover and cook over low heat for 20 more
minutes or until mixture thickens.

Serve hot with Cooked Rice (p.72).

Tip: If kafta is not ready-made, mix 1 pound lean ground beef with 1/2 onion and 1/2 bunch of parsley leaves in a
food processor. Add salt and pepper to taste.
Prepare and cook large amounts of kafta meat balls and put in freezer for up to 2 months for later use.
Instead of 1 can diced tomatoes, you can chop 4 fresh medium tomatoes.

NUTRITIONAL VALUE PER SERVING

Rich in calcium, phosphorus, zinc, and vitamin B12 (pp.126–133).

Energy (Cal)	285
Cholesterol (mg)	25
Fat (g)	6
Carbohydrate (g)	37
Protein (g)	21
Fiber (g)	1

SHISH BARAK
kafta tortellinis in yogurt soup

serves 5 | preparation time 30 min | cooking time 60 min

INGREDIENTS

1 cup all-purpose flour
1/2 teaspoon salt
2 tablespoons vegetable oil
1/4 cup water

7 ounces kafta meat

Labanyieh (Yogurt Soup)
1 cup water
4 cups fat-free plain yogurt
1 tablespoon cornstarch
1 teaspoon tahini paste
1 pinch white pepper
1 teaspoon salt
1/2 serving Cilantro and Garlic (p.10)

Tip: If kafta is not ready-made, mix 7 ounces lean
ground beef with 1/4 onion and 1/4 bunch of parsley
leaves in a food processor. Add salt and pepper to
taste.
Prepare large amounts of Shish Barak tortellinis,
divide, and put in freezer for later use.

PREPARATION

Knead flour, salt, and oil with fingertips, until
mixture becomes crumbly. Add water
gradually while kneading well, until mixture
becomes a dough.
Cover with a clean kitchen towel and leave
for 1/2 hour.
Roll dough and divide into 50 small circles
using a 2-inch cutter.

To make tortellinis, divide kafta into 50 equal
balls.
Place each kafta ball on the center of a
dough circle. Fold 1 side over the other to
make a half-moon shape, sealing the filling in
the dough.
Wrap the shape around index finger and
press the two ends together.
Arrange on baking sheet and put in
preheated oven (475°). Turn occasionally until
lightly browned, about 20–30 minutes.
Remove and set aside.

In a large pot, mix yogurt soup ingredients.
Cook over medium heat stirring constantly.
Bring to a boil.
Add tortellinis and stir for 1 more minute.

Serve hot with Cooked Rice (p.72).

Chicken & Fish

Chicken is a vital source of complete proteins, minerals (such as iron, zinc, and selenium), and vitamins B1, B2, B3, B6, and B12 (pp.126–133).

Fats are concentrated in the chicken's skin and under it; therefore, use skinless poultry and choose chicken breasts instead of the whole chicken. By removing the skin, you can cut the fat content in half. Cholesterol is in both the lean tissue and the fat in chicken.

Look for quality in fresh poultry: chicken that has creamy white to yellow skin and is free of bruises, tiny feathers, and torn or dry skin. Check for dates on food labels.

Besides being a good source of protein, fish is low in saturated fat. It also contains Omega-3 fatty acids, which offer potential heart-health benefits by reducing cholesterol and fat levels in the blood. Choose dark-colored fish such as salmon and tuna, since they are richer in fish oil than light-colored fish.

Always buy fish from a reputable source. Seafood should be displayed with food safety in mind: properly iced, well refrigerated, and in clean display cases. To save time, use properly labeled frozen fish fillets, since the nutritional value doesn't decrease with freezing, especially if frozen while fresh.

CHICKEN AND CILANTRO

serves **3** | preparation time **5 min** | soaking time **60 min** | cooking time **45 min**

INGREDIENTS

1 pound skinless chicken breasts
1 teaspoon salt
1/4 teaspoon allspice
3 tablespoons red-wine or grape vinegar
3 tablespoons vegetable oil

5 garlic cloves, crushed (p.11)
1/2 cup lemon juice
1/2 serving Cilantro and Garlic (p.10)
1 tablespoon olive oil

PREPARATION

Mix chicken with salt, allspice, vinegar, and vegetable oil.
Put in a baking dish and cover with aluminum foil. Marinate for 1 hour in the fridge.
Cook in preheated oven (475°) for 30 minutes.
Remove aluminum foil and cook until chicken is golden brown.

Mix remaining ingredients; pour over chicken.
Cook for 5 more minutes.

Serve hot with Hummus Be Tahini (p.42) or baked potatoes.

NUTRITIONAL VALUE PER SERVING

Energy (Cal)	320
Cholesterol (mg)	96
Fat (g)	15
Carbohydrate (g)	7
Protein (g)	39
Fiber (g)	1

Rich in vitamins B3, B6, and C.
Contains allylic sulfite and carotene (pp.126–133).

FATTET DAJAJ
chicken with yogurt sauce

serves 8 | preparation time 15 min | cooking time 30 min

INGREDIENTS

Rice
1 serving Cooked Ground Beef (p.9)
1 1/2 cups long-grain rice, soaked in water
    for 1/2 hour
3 cups chicken broth (p.13)
1 teaspoon salt
1 teaspoon allspice
1 teaspoon ground cinnamon

Chickpeas
4 cups water
3 cups boiled chickpeas (p.12)
2 garlic cloves, crushed (p.11)
1/2 teaspoon salt

Yogurt Sauce
4 cups fat-free plain yogurt
2 garlic cloves, crushed (p.11)
1 teaspoon tahini
1 teaspoon dried mint
1 teaspoon salt

1 pound skinless chicken breast,
    boiled (p.13) and shredded
1 medium loaf pita bread, toasted and cut
    into small squares
1 tablespoon pine nuts, toasted (p.13)

PREPARATION

Put ground beef in a large pot over high heat.
Drain rice and add to meat; stir-fry for 2 minutes.
Add chicken broth with seasonings and mix well. Bring to a boil.
Cover and cook over low heat for 30 minutes without stirring.

To prepare the chickpeas, bring water to a boil in another deep pot.
Add chickpeas, garlic, and salt, and cook over low heat until tender. Set aside.

In a separate bowl, mix yogurt sauce ingredients. Set aside.

Put hot rice in serving plate. Garnish with hot chicken and chickpeas.
Cover with bread and yogurt sauce.
Sprinkle toasted pine nuts over all.

Tip: If the meat was not previously prepared, start by cooking 5 1/4 ounces raw ground beef (p.9).
Instead of 3 cups chicken broth, use 3 cups water and 1 fat-free chicken broth cube and remove salt from the recipe.
If chickpeas were uncooked, start by boiling 1 1/2 cups dried chickpeas (p.12), or use canned chickpeas.
If the chicken breast was not previously prepared, start by boiling 1 pound (p.13).

NUTRITIONAL VALUE PER SERVING

Energy (Cal)	450
Cholesterol (mg)	50
Fat (g)	5
Carbohydrate (g)	67
Protein (g)	35
Fiber (g)	2

Rich in fiber, folate, magnesium, phosphorus, zinc, and vitamins B3, B6, and B12. Contains isoflavone (pp.126–133).

NUTRITIONAL VALUE PER SERVING

Energy (Cal)	230
Cholesterol (mg)	130
Fat (g)	4
Carbohydrate (g)	9
Protein (g)	40
Fiber (g)	2

Rich in vitamins A, B3, B6, and C.
Contains B-carotene and isoflavone (pp.126–133).

CHICKEN LOAF

serves 6 | preparation time 25 min | cooking time 60 min

INGREDIENTS

Chicken Dough
1 medium onion
2 garlic cloves
1 teaspoon salt
1/2 teaspoon white pepper
1/4 teaspoon red pepper
1/2 teaspoon cumin
1/2 teaspoon dried cilantro
2 pounds skinless chicken breast, cut
      into 5 pieces
1 egg
1/2 bunch parsley leaves

1/2 cup carrot, sliced
2 tablespoons pistachios

1 Bouquet (p.8)
1 rosemary sprig

2 tablespoons cornstarch
1/4 cup water

Tip: Prepare large amounts of chicken loaves for later use. They can be kept in the freezer for 2 months. Freeze the sauce separately.

PREPARATION

In a food processor, blend onion and garlic with seasonings. Gradually add chicken pieces until well blended.
Add egg and parsley; mix constantly until the mixture becomes a dough. Add water if needed.
Divide dough into 2 equal parts.

Roll out first portion with a wooden rolling pin into a 6x6-inch piece.
Sprinkle half the quantity of carrots and pistachios over dough. Fold over and tightly seal the edges with wet fingertips.
Repeat for the second piece of dough.

In a large nonstick pan lightly greased with oil, gently cook chicken loaves, turning them constantly until sides are browned. Cover with water.
Wrap and tie contents of Bouquet in cheesecloth, then add to pan along with rosemary. Bring to a boil.
Cover and cook over low heat for 30 more minutes.
Remove Bouquet and rosemary and set chicken broth aside in a bowl.
Cut each chicken loaf into equal slices.

Dissolve cornstarch in 1/4 cup of water.
Add to chicken broth; stir over low heat until mixture starts to thicken.
Add chicken slices. Bring to a boil.

Serve hot with Mashed Potatoes (p.70).

NUTRITIONAL VALUE PER SERVING

Energy (Cal)	540
Cholesterol (mg)	72
Fat (g)	6
Carbohydrate (g)	79
Protein (g)	43
Fiber (g)	6

Rich in fiber, folate, and vitamins B3 and B6.
Contains allylic sulfite and isoflavone (pp.126–133).

MOUGHRABIEH
chicken with pea-shaped dough

serves **8** | preparation time **15 min** | cooking time **60 min**

INGREDIENTS

2 quarts chicken broth (p.13)
2 pounds frozen moughrabieh
1 teaspoon salt
2 teaspoons allspice
2 teaspoons cumin
2 teaspoons caraway
2 teaspoons ground cinnamon
2 cups cooked chickpeas (p.12)

Sauce
1 tablespoon vegetable oil
20 pearl onions
2 cups chicken broth (p.13)

2 pounds skinless chicken breast, boiled
    (p.13) and shredded

Tip: Instead of 2 quarts chicken broth, use 2 quarts
water and 3 fat-free chicken broth cubes and remove
salt from the recipe.
If you use dried moughrabieh, allow more time for
cooking until tender.
If chickpeas were uncooked, start by boiling 3/4 cup
dried chickpeas (p.12) or use canned chickpeas.
If the chicken breast was not previously prepared,
start by boiling 2 pounds (p.13).

PREPARATION

In a large pot, bring chicken broth to a boil.
Add moughrabieh and seasonings. Stir and
boil again.
Cover and cook over low heat for 20 minutes
or until tender, stirring occasionally.
Add cooked chickpeas, cover and cook over
low heat for 10 more minutes.
Drain mixture, reserving liquid for later use.
Put drained moughrabieh and chickpeas in a
large serving dish. Keep warm while you
prepare the sauce.

To make the sauce, heat oil in a large pan,
add onions and stir-fry until lightly browned.
Onions should remain whole.
Add chicken broth and moughrabieh liquid.
Bring to a boil.
Cover and cook over low heat for 15 minutes
or until sauce thickens.
Remove onions and 1 cup sauce, add to
moughrabieh and chickpeas, and mix slowly
until evenly distributed.

Add chicken to remaining sauce in pan.
Bring to a boil.
Remove chicken and place on moughrabieh
mixture.
Add sauce according to taste.

Serve hot.

NUTRITIONAL VALUE PER SERVING

Rich in zinc and vitamins B3, B6, and B12 (pp.126–133).

Energy (Cal)	395
Cholesterol (mg)	76
Fat (g)	6
Carbohydrate (g)	50
Protein (g)	35
Fiber (g)	2

CHICKEN WITH RICE

serves **5** | preparation time **15 min** | cooking time **30 min**

INGREDIENTS

Rice

1 serving Cooked Ground Beef (p.9)
1 1/2 cups long-grain rice, soaked in water
    for 1/2 hour
3 cups chicken broth (p.13)
1 teaspoon salt
1 teaspoon allspice
1/2 teaspoon ground cinnamon

Sauce

2 cups chicken broth (p.13)
1 tablespoon all-purpose flour
1 teaspoon salt
1 teaspoon allspice
1 teaspoon ground cinnamon

1 pound skinless chicken breasts,
    boiled (p.13) and shredded
2 tablespoons pine nuts, toasted (p.13)

PREPARATION

Put ground beef in a large pot over high heat.
Drain rice and add to meat; stir for 2 minutes.
Add chicken broth and seasonings.
Bring to a boil.
Stir; cover and cook over low heat for 30 more minutes, without stirring.
Put rice on a serving plate.

In a separate pot, mix sauce ingredients and cook over low heat, stirring constantly until mixture starts to thicken.
Add chicken and bring to a boil.
Remove chicken and put on rice.
Garnish with pine nuts.
Add sauce according to taste.

Serve hot with salad or plain yogurt.

Tip: If the meat was not previously prepared, start by cooking 5 1/4 ounces raw ground beef (p.9).
If the chicken breast was not previously prepared, start by boiling 1 pound (p.13).
Instead of 3 cups chicken broth, use 3 cups water and 1 fat-free chicken broth cube and remove salt from the recipe.

MOULOUKHIEH
jew's mallow stew with chicken

serves 5 | preparation time 20 min | cooking time 45 min

INGREDIENTS

Jew's Mallow Stew
1 tablespoon vegetable oil
4 onions, finely chopped
1 1/2 quarts chicken broth (p.13)
1 teaspoon salt
1 pinch white pepper
1/2 teaspoon dried cilantro
3 pounds canned chopped Jew's mallow
1 serving Cilantro and Garlic (p.10)
1/2 cup lemon juice

1 large loaf pita bread, toasted
1 cup red-wine or grape vinegar
1 pound skinless chicken breast,
     boiled (p.13) and shredded

Cooked Rice (p.72)

PREPARATION

In a large pot, heat oil, add 1 chopped onion, and stir-fry until lightly browned.
Add chicken broth and seasonings.
Mix and bring to a boil.
Drain Jew's mallow well and add mallow to chicken broth with Cilantro and Garlic.
Stir and bring to a boil again.
Cover pan and cook over low heat for 20 minutes. Add lemon juice and cook for 5 more minutes. Set aside.

Make Cooked Rice, without vermicelli.

Cut bread into small squares.
In a small bowl, mix remaining onions and vinegar. Set aside.

Put hot rice in a serving dish; add hot chicken.
Cover with hot stew.
Garnish with bread and onion mixture.

Tip: Instead of 1 1/2 quarts chicken broth, use 1 1/2 quarts water and 2 fat-free chicken broth cubes and remove salt from the recipe.
You can also use frozen or fresh Jew's mallow.
If the chicken breast was not previously prepared, start by boiling 1 pound (p.13).

NUTRITIONAL VALUE PER SERVING

Energy (Cal)	350
Cholesterol (mg)	60
Fat (g)	5
Carbohydrate (g)	43
Protein (g)	33
Fiber (g)	7

Rich in fiber, magnesium, potassium, and vitamins A, B3, B6, C, and E. Contains caroteniods (pp.126–133).

NOUILLES
chicken tagliatelle with cream sauce

serves 8 | preparation time 30 min | cooking time 10 min

INGREDIENTS

White Sauce
1 1/2 quarts chicken broth (p.13)
10 tablespoons nonfat dry milk
6 tablespoons cornstarch
1 teaspoon salt
1/2 teaspoon white pepper
1 pinch nutmeg

1 pound tagliatelle
1 cup mushrooms, sliced
1 pound skinless chicken breast,
    boiled (p.13) and shredded

1/2 cup mozzarella cheese, grated

PREPARATION

In a saucepan, mix white sauce ingredients. Cook over low heat, stir constantly until sauce starts to thicken.

In a separate large pot, cook tagliatelle in boiling water.
Drain pasta and divide into 2 equal portions.
Put first portion in a large casserole dish.
Cover with half the white sauce.
Add chicken and mushrooms; mix well.
Add remaining tagliatelle and sauce.
Mix again.

Cover with grated cheese.
Bake in preheated oven (475°) for 20 minutes.
Broil for 5 minutes until cheese is golden brown.

Serve hot.

Tip: Instead of 1 1/2 quarts chicken broth, use 1 1/2 quarts water and 2 fat-free chicken broth cubes and remove salt from the recipe.
Or, instead of 10 tablespoons nonfat dry milk and 1 1/2 quarts chicken broth, use 3 cups fresh skim milk and 3 cups chicken broth.
If the chicken breast was not previously prepared, start by boiling 1 pound (p.13).

NUTRITIONAL VALUE PER SERVING

Energy (Cal)	430
Cholesterol (mg)	120
Fat (g)	10
Carbohydrate (g)	55
Protein (g)	30
Fiber (g)	3

Rich in vitamins B3, B6, and B12 (pp.126–133).

CHICKEN AND POTATO STEW

serves **5** | preparation time **15 min** | cooking time **35 min**

INGREDIENTS

1 tablespoon vegetable oil
1 pound chicken drumsticks
2 medium onions, finely chopped
2 garlic cloves, crushed (p.11)
1 14.5-ounce can diced tomatoes

6 medium potatoes, diced
2 cups water
1 teaspoon salt
1/2 teaspoon allspice
1/2 teaspoon ground cinnamon

PREPARATION

In a large pot, heat oil, add chicken, and
stir-fry until sides are lightly golden.
Remove and set aside.
In the same pot, add onions and stir-fry until
lightly browned.
Add garlic and stir-fry for 2 more minutes.
Add tomatoes; cook until tender.

Add remaining ingredients, plus chicken.
Cook over high heat.
Bring to a boil; stir well and cover pot.
Cook over low heat for 30 minutes or until
mixture thickens and potatoes are tender.

Serve hot with Cooked Rice (p.72).

Tip: Instead of 1 can diced tomatoes, you can chop 4 fresh medium tomatoes.
Potatoes are more nutritious if kept unpeeled because their skin is very rich in fiber, vitamins, and minerals.

NUTRITIONAL VALUE PER SERVING

Energy (Cal)	360
Cholesterol (mg)	77
Fat (g)	7
Carbohydrate (g)	51
Protein (g)	24
Fiber (g)	3

Rich in potassium and vitamins B3, B6, and C.
Contains lycopene and phenolic acids (pp.126–133).

CHICKEN LIVER

serves 3 | preparation time 5 min | soaking time 60 min | cooking time 20 min

INGREDIENTS

1 pound chicken liver
2 tablespoons soy sauce
3 tablespoons red-wine or grape vinegar
1 tablespoon yellow mustard
1/2 teaspoon salt
1 pinch white pepper
1 pinch allspice

1 tablespoon vegetable oil
5 garlic cloves, crushed (p.11)
2 tablespoons lemon juice
1 pinch parsley leaves

PREPARATION

Trim visible fat from chicken liver.
Mix soy sauce with vinegar, mustard, and seasonings. Add chicken liver.
Marinate in the fridge for 1 hour.
Drain and keep sauce for later use.

In a large pan, heat oil, add chicken liver and stir-fry for 2 minutes.
Gradually add sauce, stirring slowly until all liquid evaporates and liver is no longer pink inside. Add garlic and lemon juice.
Cover pan and cook for 1 more minute.
Garnish with parsley.

Serve hot with spaghetti or fried potatoes.

Note: You can substitute chicken breast or beef steak for the chicken liver, if desired.

Tip: This dish should be eaten in moderation because it is high in cholesterol.

NUTRITIONAL VALUE PER SERVING

Energy (Cal)	260
Cholesterol (mg)	728
Fat (g)	11
Carbohydrate (g)	10
Protein (g)	31
Fiber (g)	0

High in cholesterol, but also very rich in folate and vitamins A, B3, B6, B12, C, and K (pp.126–133).

Energy (Cal)	330
Cholesterol (mg)	97
Fat (g)	12
Carbohydrate (g)	12
Protein (g)	43
Fiber (g)	2

Rich in phosphorus and vitamins B3 and B6.
Contains allylic sulfite (pp.126–133).

SHISH TAOUK
mediterranean chicken cuts

serves **3** | preparation time **5 min** | cooking time **40 min**

INGREDIENTS

Dressing
10 garlic cloves, crushed (p.11)
1 tablespoon red-wine or grape vinegar
1/2 cup fat-free plain yogurt
2 tablespoons olive oil
1 tablespoon tomato paste
1 teaspoon allspice
1 teaspoon salt
1/4 teaspoon red pepper
1 pinch oregano

1 cup mushrooms, sliced
1 pound skinless chicken breast, diced

PREPARATION

In a bowl, mix all dressing ingredients well.
Add mushrooms and chicken and mix well.

Place in a nonstick baking dish.
Cover with aluminum foil and cook in
preheated oven (475°C) for 1 hour.
Turn every 20 minutes for even cooking.

Serve hot with Hummus Be Tahini (p.42)
and salad.

Tip: For a better taste, marinate chicken in the fridge for 4 hours before use, mixing occasionally.

NUTRITIONAL VALUE PER SERVING

Energy (Cal)	152
Cholesterol (mg)	88
Fat (g)	2
Carbohydrate (g)	0
Protein (g)	32
Fiber (g)	0

Rich in vitamins B3, B6, and B12.
Contains Omega-3 fatty acids.

BAKED FISH FILLET

serves 3 | preparation time 5 min | cooking time 30 min

INGREDIENTS

1 pound fish fillet
1 tablespoon vegetable oil
1 teaspoon salt
1/4 teaspoon white pepper
1 lemon, sliced in rounds

PREPARATION

Brush fish fillet with oil.
Sprinkle with salt and white pepper.
Add lemon slices and wrap with
aluminum foil.
Bake in preheated oven (475°)
for 30 minutes.

Serve hot with baked potatoes.

SIYADIET SAMAK
lebanese fish stew

serves **5** | preparation time **30 min** | cooking time **60 min**

INGREDIENTS

Fish Sauce
1 tablespoon vegetable oil
3 medium onions, thinly sliced
1 3/4 ounces fish
1 teaspoon cumin
1 teaspoon caraway
1 teaspoon ground cinnamon
1 teaspoon salt
2 bay leaves
2 cinnamon sticks
1/2 lemon
6 cups water

1 1/2 cups long-grain rice, soaked in water
        for 1/2 hour

1 tablespoon cornstarch
1/4 cup water
2 pounds fish fillet, baked (p.119)
3 tablespoons pine nuts, toasted (p.13)

Tip: Prepare large amounts of fish sauce for later use
in the same recipe. It can be kept in the freezer for 2
months.

PREPARATION

In a deep pot, heat oil, add onions and
stir-fry until fully brown and crispy.
Remove half the onions and set aside for
later use.
Add uncooked fish to onions in pot and stir-
fry for 3 minutes.
Add seasonings, lemon, and water.
Bring to a boil.
Cover and cook over low heat for 30 more
minutes. Drain mixture, reserving only the
liquid.

In a large pot, stir-fry drained rice for 2
minutes. Add 3 cups of the hot liquid from
previous step.
Cover and cook over low heat for 30 more
minutes. Rice should be brown in color.

Dissolve cornstarch in water.
Add to remaining liquid and stir over low
heat until sauce starts to thicken.

Put rice on a serving plate; add baked fish
and some sauce.
Garnish with pine nuts and remaining onions.

Serve hot, with salt and lemon juice if
desired.

NUTRITIONAL VALUE PER SERVING

Energy (Cal)	510
Cholesterol (mg)	96
Fat (g)	12
Carbohydrate (g)	57
Protein (g)	44
Fiber (g)	3

Rich in vitamins B3, B6, and B12.
Contains Omega-3 fatty acids (pp.126–133).

SAMKEH HARRA
spicy fish with tahini sauce

serves **5** | preparation time **20 min** | cooking time **30 min**

INGREDIENTS

Sauce
1 tablespoon vegetable oil
1 medium onion, thinly sliced
1/2 cup carrot, finely chopped
1/2 cup red bell pepper, finely chopped
1/2 cup green bell pepper, finely chopped
1 tomato, finely chopped
1/2 serving Cilantro and Garlic (p.10)
4 tablespoons tahini
4 tablespoons lemon juice
1 teaspoon salt
1/4 teaspoon white pepper
1/4 teaspoon red pepper
1 cup water

2 pounds fish fillet, baked (p.119)
1 tablespoon pine nuts, toasted (p.13)
1 pinch fresh cilantro

PREPARATION

In a large pan, heat oil, add onions, and stir-fry until lightly browned.
Add carrots and red and green bell peppers; stir-fry until tender.
Add tomato and Cilantro and Garlic and stir-fry for 5 more minutes.
In a separate bowl, mix remaining sauce ingredients, then add to vegetables, stirring constantly. Bring to a boil.
Cook over low heat for 3 more minutes, stirring constantly.

Put hot fish on a serving plate.
Add sauce.
Garnish with pine nuts and cilantro.
Add salt and lemon juice if desired.

Serve hot.

NUTRITIONAL VALUE PER SERVING

Energy (Cal)	370
Cholesterol (mg)	96
Fat (g)	15
Carbohydrate (g)	16
Protein (g)	42
Fiber (g)	3

Rich in vitamins A, B3, B6, B12, C, and K.
Contains Omega-3 fatty acids (pp.126–133).

NUTRITIONAL VALUE PER SERVING

Energy (Cal)	310
Cholesterol (mg)	76
Fat (g)	10
Carbohydrate (g)	8
Protein (g)	47
Fiber (g)	2

Rich in phosphorus and vitamins A, B3, B6, B12, and D. Contains carotenoids and Omega-3 fatty acids (pp.126–133).

BAKED SALMON

serves **5** | preparation time **10 min** | cooking time **30 min**

INGREDIENTS

7 ounces salmon, cut into 5 slices
1 tablespoon vegetable oil
1 teaspoon salt
1 teaspoon white pepper
1 leek, thinly sliced
1 cup celery, thinly sliced
2 carrots, thinly sliced

PREPARATION

Brush fish with oil, then sprinkle with salt and white pepper.
Wrap in aluminum foil with vegetables.
Cook in preheated oven (475°) for 30 minutes.
Remove aluminum foil.

Serve hot with lemon juice and baked potatoes.

NUTRITIONAL
INFORMATION

ENERGY

Calories are units of energy. The term "calorie" describes both the amount of energy in food and the amount of energy the body uses. The body's need for energy never stops.
Three nutrients – carbohydrate, fat, and protein – as well as alcohol supply energy, measured in calories, in food.

Source of Energy	Calories per gram
Fat	9
Alcohol	7
Carbohydrate	4
Protein	4

These nutrients are released from food during digestion, then absorbed in the bloodstream and converted to glucose, or blood sugar, after a long process in the digestive system. This energy is used to perform all bodily functions, both involuntary (mental effort, breathing, digestion, vision) and voluntary (walking, athletics).
Age, sex, basal metabolic rate, body size, physical condition, and activity level all contribute to how much energy an individual needs. Healthy individuals need between 1,800 and 3,000 calories.
- 1,800 calories is about right for many sedentary women and some older adults. Young children need a variety of foods, but may need fewer than 1,800 calories.
- 2,200 calories meets the needs of most children, teenage girls, active women, and many sedentary men. Women who are pregnant and breastfeeding may need more.
- 2,800 calories is about right for teenage boys, many active men, and some very active women.

The numbers given in the nutritional value sections of each recipe are approximate calculated values of energy per serving.

PROTEIN

Protein supplies amino acids, which are the building blocks that build, repair, and maintain body tissues.
As a nutrient, protein performs many functions. It is a part of every cell in the body and a constant supply is necessary to repair cells as they wear out. During times of growth – infancy, childhood, adolescence, and pregnancy – the body needs protein to make new body tissues.
Protein also helps regulate body processes. As enzymes and hormones, proteins make various chemical reactions happen. As antibodies, they protect you from disease-carrying bacteria and viruses.
Protein also supplies your body with energy if you don't consume enough from carbohydrates and fat. Otherwise, protein can be saved for its unique function: to build and repair body tissue. When you consume more protein than you need, it's broken down and stored as body fat, not as a reserve supply of protein.
15% of one's daily energy intake should come from protein, around 70 grams per 2,000 calories.

FAT

Fats in food have a number of nutritional functions. They serve as a concentrated source of energy and a source of essential fatty acids. They act as carriers of fat-soluble vitamins – A, D, E, and K – and affect the palatability of foods. Body fat, also known as adipose tissues, is where extra energy is stored. It also serves to protect the body from injury and to provide insulation from cold weather.

Fats are of several types:
• Saturated fats, which are firm at room temperature, include butter, coconut oil, and palm oil and are also found in red meats and chicken. They are generally unhealthy because they increase the cholesterol level in the blood, even if they are cholesterol free.
• Unsaturated fats, which include oils derived from canola, olives, corn, sunflowers, and rape seeds, are generally healthy; they increase the good cholesterol (HDL) in the blood, and slightly decrease the bad cholesterol (LDL).
• Omega-3 fatty acids – polyunsaturated fatty acids of a somewhat different structure – are found mostly in seafood, especially higher-fat, cold-water varieties such as mackerel, albacore tuna, salmon, sardines, and lake trout. Both soybean oil and canola oil supply some Omega-3s, too. Some research, although inconclusive, suggests that Omega-3s may help prevent blood platelets from clotting and sticking to artery walls, and so may help lower the risk for blocked blood vessels and heart attacks. Omega-3s may also help prevent arteries from hardening.
• Hydrogenated fats are unsaturated fats that are processed (by adding hydrogen molecules) to make them stable and solid at room temperature. Through processing the fat is made more saturated and is called trans-fatty acids. It becomes more harmful, increasing LDL and decreasing HDL.

25–30% of daily energy intake should be from fats, around 60–65 grams per 2000 calories. Choose polyunsaturated over hydrogenated or trans-fatty acids.

CHOLESTEROL

Cholesterol is a fat-like substance, but it is not a fat itself and does not have any calories. Cholesterol is only found in foods of animal origin and has a different structure from fat. It has several necessary functions in the body, such as creating cells, especially nerve and brain cells. However, too much cholesterol in the bloodstream is linked to heart disease.

The cholesterol that circulates in your body comes from two sources:
• Foods and beverages of animal origin, such as eggs, meat, chicken, fish, and dairy products. Foods derived from plants do not contain cholesterol, but still may increase cholesterol levels. For example, coconut oil is cholesterol free because it is made from a plant, but it is still rich in saturated fats, which increase blood cholesterol.
• The liver and most of the tissues in the human body can make cholesterol to satisfy their needs. Therefore, high blood cholesterol can be the result of internal production and not necessarily from food.

Daily food intake should provide less than 300 milligrams of cholesterol.

CARBOHYDRATES

Carbohydrates are the body's main source of energy, powering everything from jogging to breathing to digesting food. Glucose, known as blood sugar, is the main form of carbohydrate used for energy in the body, especially the brain.

Carbohydrates are classified into two groups:
• Simple carbohydrates, highly absorbable and easy to digest, are found in white sugar, fruit juice, sweets; they are usually called "empty calories" because they provide energy and no nutrients.
• Complex carbohydrates are slow to be digested and absorbed, and are made up from many sugar units; examples are pasta, potatoes, rice, beans. They are usually nutrient dense, supplying vitamins, minerals, and fiber.

55% of daily energy intake, or around 270 grams per 2000 calories, should come from carbohydrates, mostly complex carbohydrates.

FIBER

The term fiber refers to the complex carbohydrates in fruit, vegetables, grains, nuts, and legumes that can't be broken down by human digestive enzymes and therefore are calorie free. Meat and dairy products do not contain fiber.

There are two basic types of fiber:
• Soluble fiber is found in grains and some fruits and vegetables. It may help reduce blood cholesterol levels, thereby reducing the risk of heart disease and may also help control the rise in blood-sugar levels following a meal, which is important for people with diabetes.
• Insoluble fiber is found in fruit and vegetable skins, nuts, and grains, especially wheat. It creates a feeling of fullness and adds bulk to the contents of the colon and relief from constipation. It may decrease the risk of colon and rectal cancers.

MINERALS

15 minerals have been identified as nutritionally necessary; a part of every body tissue, they are essential to life. Minerals help chemical reactions take place in the body and provide structure in the form of bones and teeth. The human body cannot produce them. They are calorie free and make up only about 4% of body weight.

• The "major" minerals include those we need the most: calcium, phosphorus, magnesium, chloride, potassium, and sodium. These last three are called electrolytes; together they help regulate fluid in the body and transmit nerve or electrical impulses.
• The "trace" minerals include chromium, copper, fluoride, iodine, iron, manganese, molybdenum, selenium, and zinc.

Major Minerals

Calcium
Food Sources: Dairy products, dark green leafy vegetables, fish with edible bones, legumes, seeds, and nuts.
Functions:
The most abundant mineral in the body, especially in bones and teeth.
Helps muscle movement and regulates heartbeat.
Plays an important role in the function of nerves.
Helps blood to coagulate.

Phosphorus
Food Sources: Milk, meat, poultry, fish, eggs, legumes, nuts, bread and baked foods.
Functions:
A major component of bones and teeth.
Helps produce energy in the body.
Plays a vital role in regulating energy in the organs.
A component of DNA and RNA.

Magnesium
Food Sources: Legumes, nuts, whole grains, and green vegetables.
Functions:
An important part of 300 enzymes that regulate body functions.
Produces energy, builds proteins, and helps in muscle contractions.
Maintains nerve and muscle cells.
Fights sleep disorders, depression, and fatigue.
Plays an important role in maintaining teeth and bones.

Major Minerals: Electrolytes

Chloride
Food Sources: Table salt.

Functions:

Helps regulate fluids inside and outside body cells.

A component of stomach acid, which helps digest food and absorb nutrients.

Helps transmit nerve impulses.

Potassium

Food Sources: Apricots, avocados, bananas, cantaloupe, grapefruit, kiwi, oranges, strawberries, tomatoes, potatoes, dried fruit, fresh meat, poultry, and fish.

Functions:

Helps regulate fluids and mineral balance inside and outside body cells.

Helps maintain normal blood pressure.

Helps in the transmission of nerve signals.

Helps in muscle movement.

Sodium

Food Sources:

About 75% of the sodium we eat is from processed foods; the remaining 25% comes from table salt. A small amount occurs naturally in food.

Functions:

Helps regulate fluids and mineral balance inside and outside body cells.

Helps transmit nerve impulses.

Regulates blood pressure.

Helps in muscle relaxation, including the heart.

Trace Minerals

Chromium

Food Sources: Meat, whole grains, and nuts.

Functions:

Works with insulin to help the body use glucose (blood sugar).

Copper

Food Sources: Organ meats, especially liver; seafood, nuts, and seeds.

Functions:

An essential component of enzymes.

Helps in creating hemoglobin, which transports oxygen throughout the body.

Helps in producing energy.

Fluoride

Food Sources: Fish with edible bones (such as canned salmon), and tea.

Functions:

Strengthens teeth and protects against cavities.

Helps prevent osteoporosis.

Iodine

Food Sources: Saltwater fish, fortified table salt.

Functions:

Part of thyroxin (thyroid hormone), which regulates the rate at which the body uses energy.

Iron

Food Sources: Heme iron from animal sources, including meat, liver, poultry, and salmon.

Non-heme iron from plant sources as spinach, chard, prune juice, dried apricots; legumes such as lentils, beans, soybeans, nuts.

Heme iron is absorbed better than non-heme iron in the human body. Non-heme iron absorption can be enhanced by

consuming it with foods high in vitamin C.
Functions:
Forms hemoglobin in the red blood cells; hemoglobin carries oxygen throughout the body.
Fights anemia, fatigue, and infections.

Manganese
Food Sources: Whole grain products, pineapple, kale, strawberries, and tea.
Functions:
A component of many enzymes.

Molybdenum
Food Sources: Milk, legumes, bread and grain products.
Functions:
A component of many enzymes.
Works with riboflavin to incorporate iron into hemoglobin for red blood cells.

Selenium
Food Sources: Seafood, liver, kidney, grain products, and seeds.
Functions:
Works as an antioxidant with vitamin E to protect cells from damage that may lead to cancer, heart disease, and other problems.
Aids in cell growth.

Zinc
Food Sources: Meat, liver, and seafood are the best sources; also whole-grain products such as wheat bran, legumes, and soybeans.
Functions:
Essential for growth; a component of 70 different enzymes.
Promotes cell reproduction, tissue growth and repair, and wound healing.
Helps the body use carbohydrate, protein, and fat.

VITAMINS

13 vitamins have been identified as nutritionally necessary; they work with other nutrients to help perform a variety of functions. Vitamins are also called micronutrients because they are needed in only tiny amounts. The human body cannot produce them. They are calorie-free.

Vitamins are divided into 2 groups: water soluble and fat soluble. The group name describes how they are carried in food and transported in the body.
• Fat-soluble vitamins include vitamins A, D, E, and K.
• Water-soluble vitamins include vitamin C and the B-vitamins: thiamin (B1), riboflavin (B2), niacin, vitamin B6, folate, vitamin B12, biotin, and pantothenic acid.

Fat-Soluble Vitamins

Vitamin A
Food Sources: Liver, fish oil, eggs, and milk.
Carotenoids are converted in the body to vitamin A. Carotenoids are found in spinach, collards, kale, broccoli, carrots, peaches, pumpkin, sweet potatoes, red peppers, and cantaloupes.
Functions:
Strengthens vision, especially night vision.
Promotes the growth and health of all cells, tissues, bones, and teeth.
Protects against infection by keeping the skin and tissues healthy.
Protects against several diseases, especially cancer.

Vitamin D (Calciferol)

Food Sources: Cheese, eggs, some fish (sardines and salmon), fortified milk, breakfast cereals, and margarine.

Vitamin D is known as the "sunshine vitamin" because the body can make it after exposure to sunlight or ultraviolet lights.

Functions:

Maintains the calcium–phosphorus exchange in the body.

Helps in forming bones and teeth.

Prevents osteoporosis.

Vitamin E (Tocopherol)

Food Sources: Vegetable oils, margarine, salad dressings, seeds, nuts, and wheat germ.

Functions:

Works as an antioxidant.

May help protect against illnesses, including heart disease and some types of cancer.

Vitamin K

Food Sources: Parsley, spinach, broccoli, dairy products, meat, eggs, and cereals.

Intestinal bacteria produce some of the vitamin K we need.

Functions:

Helps in forming proteins that encourage blood to clot.

Water-Soluble Vitamins

Vitamin C (Ascorbic Acid)

Food Sources: Citrus fruits, berries, melons, peppers, many dark green leafy vegetables, potatoes, and tomatoes.

Functions:

Helps in creating collagen, which connects muscles, bones, and tissues.

Helps the body absorb iron from plant sources of food.

Prevents tissue oxidization, which lowers the risk of getting cancer and heart disease.

Helps form and repair red blood cells, bones and other tissues, and helps keep capillary walls and blood vessels firm.

Important for healthy gums and to heal cuts and wounds.

Prevents infection by keeping the immune system healthy.

Vitamin B1 (Thiamin)

Food Sources: Bread, rice, pasta, tortillas, fortified breakfast cereals, pork, liver, and other variety meats.

Functions:

Helps cells produce energy from carbohydrates.

Builds and repairs nerve and muscle tissue.

Prevents loss of appetite.

Vitamin B2 (Riboflavin)

Food Sources: Liver, kidney, heart, dairy products, enriched bread, cereal, eggs, meat, green leafy vegetables, and nuts.

Functions:

Helps all cells produce energy from proteins.

Helps change tryptophan (an amino acid) into niacin (vitamin B3).

Maintains hair and nails.

Facilitates the function of the nervous system.

Vitamin B3 (Niacin)

Food Sources: Poultry, fish, beef, peanut butter, and legumes.

Some vitamin B3 is produced in the body from tryptophan (an amino acid).

Functions:

Helps all cells produce energy from carbohydrates and fats.

Helps enzymes function in the body.

Maintains healthy skin.
Helps digestion.
Protects the nervous system.

Vitamin B6 (Pyridoxine)
Food Sources: Chicken, fish, pork, liver, kidney, whole grains, nuts, and legumes.
Functions:
Helps produce other body chemicals, such as insulin, hemoglobin, and antibiotics, to fight infection.
Helps all cells produce energy from proteins.
Helps in transporting amino acids.
Helps in creating vitamin B3.
Facilitates the function of the nervous system.

Folate (Folic Acid)
Food Sources: Leafy vegetables, orange juice, some fruits, legumes, liver, yeasted breads, wheat germ, bread, cereal, rice, and pasta products.
Functions:
Plays an essential role in producing DNA and RNA to make new cells.
Works with vitamin B12 to form hemoglobin in red blood cells.
Prevents heart disease.
Lowers risk of neural tube defects in newborns.

Vitamin B12
Food Sources: Meat, fish, poultry, eggs, milk, breakfast cereals, and some fortified foods.
Functions:
Works with folate to make red blood cells.
Serves in every cell as a vital part of many chemicals.
Helps the body use fatty acids and some amino acids.
Facilitates the function of the nervous system.

Biotin
Food Sources: Eggs, liver, yeasted breads, and cereals.
Functions:
Helps all body cells produce energy from protein, fats, and carbohydrates.

Pantothenic Acid
Food Sources: Meat, poultry, fish, whole grain cereals, legumes, and milk.
Functions:
Helps all body cells produce energy from protein, fats, and carbohydrates.

PHYTOCHEMICALS

Plants naturally produce these chemicals to protect themselves against viruses, bacteria, and fungi. They also provide color, flavor, and scent. Recent scientific studies have proven that they could help in protecting humans against some diseases, such as heart disease and cancer, as indicated below:

Allylic Sulfite
Food Sources: Garlic and onions.
Functions: Helps in removing toxins that cause cancer.

B-Carotene (Beta-Carotene)
Food Sources: Carrots, apricots, peaches, and zucchinis.
Functions: Helps protect the immune system.

Carotenoids
Food Sources: Dark green and orange-colored plants such as parsley, Jew's mallow, chicory, spinach, chard, etc.
Functions: Prevents toxic molecules from invading and damaging cells.
An anti-inflammatory, which lowers the risk of some cancers.

Cumarin
Food Sources: Turmeric, curry, mustard, and saffron.
Functions: An antioxidant that helps prevent heart disease and cancer.

Gingerol
Food Sources: Ginger.
Functions: An antioxidant that helps prevent heart disease and cancer.

Isoflavone
Food Sources: Beans, peas, peanuts, and tofu.
Functions: May reduce the risk of breast and ovarian cancer.

Isothiocyanates, Indoles
Food Sources: Cabbage, broccoli, kale, and cauliflower.
Functions: Blocks carcinogens from damaging cells; interferes with the action of a precancerous form of estrogen.

Lutein
Food Sources: Spinach.
Functions: Reduces blindness in the elderly.

Lycopene
Food Sources: Tomatoes, especially cooked, and kiwi.
Functions: May decrease the risk of prostate cancer.

Omega-3 Fatty Acids
Food Sources: Fish oil, mackerel, salmon, and trout.
Functions: May decrease the risk of heart disease.

Phenolic Acids
Food Sources: Potato, apple, blueberry, cherry, orange, grapefruit, and coffee beans.
Functions: An antioxidant that may prevent some cancers.

Tannins
Food Sources: Lentils, black-eyed peas, fava beans, and grape and apple juices.
Functions: An antioxidant that may prevent some cancers.

Zeaxanthin
Food Sources: Kale, mustard, horseradish, and corn.
Functions: An antioxidant that enhances immune function and may prevent some cancers.

GLOSSARY

Allspice, *Bihar helou*

Artichoke, *Ardichaouki*

Asparagus, *Halioun*

Basil, *Habak*

Basil, dried, *Habak yabes*

Bay leaves, *Warak ghar*

Beef kafta, *Kafta bakar*

Beef steak, slices, *Steak bakar sharaeh*

Beef steak, sirloin, *Steak fofillet*

Bell pepper, green, *Fleifleh khadra*

Bell pepper, red, *Fleifleh hamra*

Black lentils, *Adas aswad*

Black pepper, *Bhar aswad*

Bulgur, *Burghol*

Bulgur, coarse, *Burghol khishen*

Bulgur, fine, *Burghol naem*

Cabbage, *Malfouf*

Caraway powder, *Karawyah Boudra*

Cardamom, *Habbat al hal*

Cardamom, crushed, *Habb el hal madkuk*

Cauliflower, *Karnabit*

Celery, *Krafis*

Chard, *Salek*

Chicken broth, *Marak al dajaj*

Chicken liver, *Kasbet dajaj*

Chickpeas, *Hummus habb*

Chicory, *Hendbah*

Cinnamon stick, *Oud Kerfeh*

Cinnamon, ground, *Kerfeh naema*

Cilantro, *Kezbara Tazajah*

Cilantro and garlic, *Kezbara wa toum*

Cilantro, dried, *Kezbara yabisa*

Corn, *Doura*

Cornstarch, *Nashaa*

Cracked wheat, *Burghol*

Crystal salt, *Maleh khishen*

Cumin, *Kammoun*

Eggplant, *Bazenjan*

Fava beans, *Ful*

Flour, *Tahin*

Flour, white, *Tahin abiad*

Garlic bulb, *Kouz toum*

Garlic clove, *Fass toum*

Ginger, *Zanjabeel tazaj*

Jew's mallow, *Mouloukhieh*

Keshek, *Keshek*

Kidney beans, *Fassoulieh*

Kidney beans, red, *Fassoulieh hamra*

Kidney beans, white, *Fassoulieh baida*

Leek, *Karrat*

Lentil, *Adas*

Lima beans, *Loubieh khadra*

Marjoram, *Mardakoush*

Mastic, *Messek*

Meat, blended, *Lahem madkouk*

Meat, diced, *Lahem ras asfour*

Meat, minced, *Lahem mafroom*

Mint, dried, *Naanaa yabes*

Mushroom, *Feter*

Mustard, yellow, *Khardal asfar*

Nutmeg, *Jouz el tib*

Okra, *Bemiah*

Parsley, *Bakdouness*

Pear, green, *Bazella khadra*

Pine nuts, *Sanawbar*

Pita bread, *Khobez Arabi*

Radish, *Fejel*

Raisins, yellow, dried, *Zbeeb asfar*

Red beans, *Fassoulieh hamra*

Red pepper, *Bhar ahmar*

Rice, long-grain, *Roz amariki, tawil*

Rice, short-grain, *Roz massri, kassir*

Rosemary stick, *Eklil al jabal*

Saffron, *Zaafaran oroppi*

Shrimp, *Kraydess*

Sumac, *Summac*

Tahini, *Tahini*

Tomato paste, *Robb al banadoura*

Tomato sauce, *Salsat al banadoura*

Vermicelli, *Shaayriah*

Vinegar, red, *Khall inab*

Watercress, *Baklah*

White pepper, *Bhar abiad*

Zucchini, *Kousa*

TIME TABLE & NUTRITIONAL VALUES

	Page	Preparation (min)	Cooking (min)	Serves	Energy (Cal)	Cholesterol (mg)	Fat (g)	Carbohydrate (g)	Protein (g)	Fiber (g)
Adas Be Hamod	30	25	40	6	215	-	3	37	10	7
Artichoke Stew	71	5	30	4	210	27	7	17	20	7
Baba Ghannuj	42	15	15	3	205	-	14	16	4	2
Baked Fish Fillet	119	5	30	3	152	88	2	-	32	-
Baked Salmon	125	10	30	5	310	76	10	8	47	2
Balila	27	5	15	4	415	0	17	50	16	6
Burghol Be Dfin	62	5	30	5	445	22	8	67	26	16
Bulgur with Tomato	53	10	40	3	290	-	6	51	8	11
Chicken and Cilantro	100	5	45	3	320	96	15	7	39	1
Chicken and Potato Stew	114	15	35	5	360	77	7	51	24	3
Chicken with Rice	109	15	30	5	395	76	6	50	35	2
Chicken Liver	116	5	20	3	260	728	11	10	31	-
Chicken Loaf	105	25	60	6	230	130	4	9	40	2
Chicken Soup	36	5	35	5	270	80	5	32	25	1
Cooked Rice	72	5	15	6	240	-	-	55	5	1
Dawood Basha	95	15	50	5	190	54	8	9	20	1
Eggplant Salad	21	15	6	4	190	-	14	14	2	2
Fattet Dajaj	102	15	30	8	450	50	5	67	35	2
Fattet Hummus	44	10	20	5	500	4	7	80	30	12
Fattoush	18	25	-	5	225	-	14	21	4	3
Ful Mudammas	27	5	15	3	460	-	19	53	19	11
Green Bean Salad	22	5	15	5	210	-	14	17	4	7
Green Beans in Tomato Sauce	51	25	45	4	190	-	4	32	6	7
Green Pea Stew	76	5	30	4	260	27	8	26	21	5
Hummus Be Tahini	42	5	15	5	330	-	18	32	10	8
Kafta and Potatoes	92	20	40	4	380	75	8	45	32	7
Kebbe in a Pan	85	30	50	8	390	60	12	45	29	11
Kebbe Labanyieh	83	30	60	5	380	41	5	56	28	7
Keshek	35	5	10	4	375	45	11	50	19	10
Kidney Bean Salad	25	5	15	4	360	-	15	42	15	14
Kidney Bean Stew	78	10	30	6	350	18	5	49	27	14
Kidney Beans in Tomato Sauce	40	10	30	6	330	-	3	57	18	15
Laban Emmo	75	10	15	5	225	26	6	19	23	1

Makhluta	31	10	60	6	325	-	4	55	17	18
Mashed Potatoes	70	10	30	4	200	-	-	43	7	3
Meatloaf with Eggs	67	20	40	5	280	185	18	6	23	1
Mehshi Katei	50	30	60	5	250	-	4	47	7	13
Moudardara	49	5	45	4	330	-	8	52	12	15
Moughrabieh	107	15	60	8	540	72	6	79	43	6
Moujadara	52	15	40	3	280	-	5	45	14	13
Mouloukhieh	110	20	45	5	350	60	5	43	33	7
Moussaka	47	10	60	4	260	-	6	42	10	9
Nouilles	112	30	10	8	430	120	10	55	30	3
Okra Stew	74	10	30	4	215	27	7	19	19	4
Oven-Baked Omelet	58	15	30	4	280	330	11	27	18	3
Potato and Egg Salad	28	10	30	4	290	185	12	36	9	3
Rishta	32	10	30	4	275	-	4	46	14	6
Roast Beef	68	20	90	5	470	103	19	29	46	4
Samkeh Harra	122	20	30	5	370	96	15	16	42	3
Shawarma	65	10	50	5	510	96	29	14	48	3
Sheikh el Mehshi	89	15	90	5	205	36	7	19	17	6
Shepherd's Pie	86	20	50	8	370	51	9	57	16	5
Shish Barak	97	30	60	5	285	25	6	37	21	1
Shish Taouk	118	5	40	3	330	97	12	12	43	2
Siyadiet Samak	120	30	60	5	510	96	12	57	44	3
Spinach Stew	90	5	15	4	190	22	9	13	14	6
Stir-Fried Chicory with Onions	55	30	15	5	145	-	9	13	3	11
Stuffed Zucchinis	80	30	60	5	195	18	2	32	12	5
Tabbouleh	16	30	-	5	200	-	13	18	4	6
White Spaghetti	56	10	30	6	420	30	6	72	20	2
Zucchini Omelet	82	5	30	5	230	290	12	8	22	1

INDEX

WHERE TO FIND INGREDIENTS

The list below includes a selection of places where you can purchase specialty Lebanese ingredients that may not be available at your local supermarket.

Dayna's Market
www.daynasmarket.com
26300 Ford Rd. - Suite 415
Dearborn Heights, MI 48127
tel: 1-888-5-DAYNAS (1-888-532-9627)
info@daynasmarket.com
A wide selection of grains, herbs and spices (including mastic, sumac, and zaatar), legumes, and nuts. Also carries tahini, rose water, and orange water.

Shamra's
www.shamra.com
2650 University Blvd.
Wheaton, MD 20902
tel: (301) 942-9726
fax: (240) 337-6468
info@shamra.com
Carries herbs and spices, rose and orange water, canned mouloukhieh or Jew's Mallow (search for "mloukhiyeh"), and a large selection of Middle Eastern coffees.

Buy Lebanese
BuyLebanese.com
tel: +961-3-602405
info@buylebanese.com
Carries keshek powder, dried mouloukhieh (search for "mloukhieh"), various infused waters and syrups, and a selection of fresh sweets and breads.

Lebanese Products & Hookahs
Lebaneseproducts.com
tel: +961-3-473376
sales@lebaneseproducts.com
A broad variety of items, including canned mouloukhieh (search for "mloukhieh"), keshek powder (search for "kishek"), and hard-to-find spices.